David Swann

The Privilege of Rain

Time Among the Sherwood Outlaws

First published in 2010
by Waterloo Press (Hove)
95 Wick hall
Furze Hill
Hove BN3 1PF

Printed in Palatino 10.7pt by
One Digital
54 Hollingdean Road
East Sussex BN2 4AA

A CIP record for this book is available
from the British Library

ISBN 978-1-906742-09-6

By the same author

The Last Days of Johnny North (Elastic Press, 2006)
Subtraction (Spitfire Press, 2005)

Editor

Mouth Ogres, co-edited with Hugh Dunkerley
(Oxmarket Press, 2001)
Dreaming Beasts, co-edited with Hugh Dunkerley
(Krebs & Snopes, 2005)
Beyond the Wall: Words Set Free From Prison
(HMP Nottingham, 1998)

Acknowledgements

Work from this book has appeared in: *Agenda, Nottingham Poetry International, Saturday Night Desperate, Samizdat, Staple, Timbila, The Interpreter's House, Generosity: an Anthology*, several *Lancaster Literature Festival* anthologies, *The Sensitively Thin Bill of the Shag, The Interpreter's House, The Slab 2, The Slab of Fun, The Last Days of Johnny North* (Elastic Press), *The Illustrated Brighton Moment*, Duke of York's Poetry Posters, and *Texts' Bones*. Poems have won prizes in the following competitions: Bedford Open, Pitshanger Open, Osaka Haiku Open (Japan). Material has been performed through: BBC South East, BBC East Midlands, Amsterdam University, Short Fuse, The South, Staffordshire Literature Festival, Tongues & Strings, World Spirit, Grit Lit, and The Brighton Moment.

The Arts Council of England funded the residency at HMP Nottingham. The following organisations showed willing: University of Chichester, Lancaster University, East Midlands Arts, Waterloo Press, Writers in Prison Network, and The South. Helpful individuals in positions of responsibility included: Jago Morrison, Sue Morgan, Diana Barsham, Jan Ainsley, Isla Duncan, Peter Bennett, Richard Branch, Alistair Niven, Linda Anderson, Clive Hopwood, and Gordon Todd & his inspiring colleagues in the Education and Library Departments. I am grateful to all.

This book was shaped by the wise, insightful editing of Naomi Foyle. I am also fortunate to have been guided and inspired by Chris Jones, John O'Donoghue, and Clare Dunne. I am likewise indebted to workshop advice from: Hugh Dunkerley, Henry Shukman, Jemma Kennedy, Karen Stevens, Lorna Thorpe, Bethan Roberts, Jane Rusbridge, Kate Betts, Vicki Feaver, Stephanie Norgate, James Simpson, Kai Merriott, Mick Jackson, Nick Warburton, Mimi Khalvati, Brendan Cleary, Robert Dickinson, Andrew Dilger, Christopher North, Jackie Wills.

I acknowledge help from these folk during the evolution of this book: my parents, Steven Swann, Rachel Hughes, James Ebdon, Anke Mittelberg, David Hesmondhalgh, Helen Steward, Tony Crockford, Andrew Hook, John Davies, Simon Jenner, Alan Morrison, Matilda Persson, Mike Usiskin, Simon Finch, Pete Barnes, Martin Elvins, Greg Challis, David Gilliver, Jeannette Laouadi, Andrea Birkin, Roger Rees,

David Clee, Joe Wells, Bran Nicol, Ian Worden, Jess de Mellow, Keiren Phelan, Tom Cunliffe, Tricia Harewood, Andre Mangeot, Jens Haus, Peter Knaggs, Daithidh MacEochaidh, The Serenity, Alison MacLeod, Susanna Jones, Ben Noys, Julie Hesmondhalgh, Ian Kershaw, Matt Clegg, Kerrith Bell, Steve Haywood, Stewart Wills, Linda Chase, Sue Shorter, Brian Turner, David Craig, Alan Burns, Janice Fitzpatrick Simmons & the late Jimmy Simmons, Phil & Amanda Grabsky, the Vermond family (Truus, Ellen, Karin, Mirjam, Rian, Tim, Lisa, Merel, Sam, Lasse), Danny Verbeek, and Jan Willem Sligting. Also: Pamela & the late Robert Woof, who opened the road, and Tom Melk, Sarah Potter, Andy Paczos, & Jonathan Carr, who brought me home. Unfortunately, it takes me a decade to write these things; if I have overlooked anyone's kindness, please forgive me. I blame Time's ravages.

Last, not least: Angela Vermond.

In memory of Piet Vermond, the best and kindest of men.

Contents

Seed

Sap

Stump

*With gratitude
to Gordon Todd and his colleagues,
and all the prisoners and officers
who taught me about freedom.*

*Also, to Joanne Swann & Johnny Rowley,
who offered shelter.*

Never saw the East coast
until I moved to the West

Tom Waits

The Privilege of Rain

Time Among the Sherwood Outlaws

Seed

The prison has one beautiful tree

The prison has one beautiful tree:
it droops blossom for two weeks each year.
Then the wind comes in like a robber,
stuffs its pockets with colour,
and goes where three hundred men
yearn to follow.

First day

On the way in, I had counted the gates as they were locked behind us. Five gates, six...

My boss swung the final gate shut as an unseen double-decker growled past on the road beyond the wall. That's how close the world was. How far away. Just seven gates...

I was led into the education block, passing a cluster of unyielding men who had gathered in the dog-leg of the corridor. I didn't know who was a prisoner and who wasn't. Their clothes were made of drab acrylic. Against my expectations, only one of the men seemed to be wearing anything that I understood as a prison uniform. He was dressed in navy clothes with bright yellow stripes down the sides.

Secretly, I practised holding the keys in my pocket. There were only two of them. Two keys. You'd to shield the keys from forgers, that's what the head of security had told me. Some forgers needed only ten seconds to memorise the cut.

'The thing is,' I said, rushing to keep up, 'is, I thought there'd be *tons* of keys...'

My boss nodded. 'These two keys fit almost every lock in this whole place. That's why you've to hand them in at the gate whenever you leave the jail...'

In the corridor, a cluster of men stopped to study me. The keys burned against my thigh. Their chain might as well have been connected to the anchor of a trawler. I'd never felt more giddy, was almost floating on a wave of my own fear. But heavy too. Both at the same time. Anchored. Adrift.

'If you forget... if you leave the prison with those two keys... they'll have no choice but to change all the locks,' said my boss.

His voice slowed to a crawl.

'Every. Single. Lock. In. This. Jail.'

That first morning, I was allowed to sit in on various lessons. To get a flavour of how things went.

First I was shown the cookery class. On the way in, I noticed a blackboard covered with hooks, where the prisoners hung their tools. Each tool belonged in a particular place, and each spot on the board was marked with a white outline of the tool, like the lines painted around bodies on TV cop shows.

I noticed that several knives were missing from their hooks.

Over by the cookers, a group of men in aprons had almost finished melting chocolate to pour over Rice Krispies clustered in bun cases.

The teacher shrugged. 'A special request,' she said. 'I was supposed to be showing 'em roast beef, but...'

All around her, prisoners stared into the pans as if they could see naked women down there in the depths, faces simultaneously animated and stunned.

'Not the spoons,' the teacher scalded. 'Don't lick the spoons yet!'

Some of the men cracked up laughing. 'You can't help yourself,' one of them offered. 'It's the temptation...'

The teacher directed a smile into the pockets of her apron, where no-one might see it, where it might be safe.

Later, a quietness fell over the room as the men sated themselves on their buns and their spoons.

'Happiness...' I said to the teacher.

'Or caffeine, lad.'

'Happiness IS caffeine, isn't it?' said one of the men. 'Or did I miss summat? Have I been in here too long to remember the difference?'

The teacher waved him away. 'Philosophy's in that classroom over there,' she said. 'This is cookery, lad. Wipe down your work surfaces.'

'Yes, Miss,' said the prisoner.

Nervous in the staff-room at lunchtime, I listened to the conversations of the teachers around me. Their voices contained that strange mixture of exhaustion and wonder that I'd known from my own days as a teacher. But the things they discussed I barely understood at all.

'... the poisoner?'

'So they say. Still up to his old tricks. Even in here...'

'How?'

'Slipping it into folks' drinks, so they reckon. Cups of coffee, and that...'

Both teachers turned suddenly, realising that I was staring at them.

One of them smiled wearily. 'Fancy a brew, lad?'

I was told it was time to go on the wing. I thought of the pigeons I'd seen in a dingy alcove near the Governor's office. The places a creature may choose to spend its freedom! *On the wing, on the wing.* Every phrase hit me in the stomach.

I was put in the care of a man who'd been mopping a landing on the 3s before we interrupted him. He'd show me the ropes, my boss said. He was a trusted prisoner. I nodded, confused. From a distance, I'd again mistaken the man for a civvie.

The trusted man had dull eyes, dark waxy rings beneath them. But the ghost of a smile came easily to his face, and that was a relief because the smile softened his features and seemed to grant him respite from the gloom that had seeped out from his eyes. He took me along the landing, grunting hello's to men who didn't look up. Would I like a drink of coffee, he asked? He had a flask on the go; would I fancy a drink of coffee?

I thought about the teachers' lunchtime poison stories. I also worked hard to remember advice offered by a friend, an actress: *Don't blink at the wrong moment. If you're challenged, do a Michael Caine on them. Power is control over the eye. Power is not blinking.*

That first week, I must have looked deranged. I didn't blink again until January. I started to understand why the men's eyes burned.

I did my Michael Caine. 'Yes,' I said to the trusted prisoner, probably shaking my head, 'I'd really like a drink of coffee. Very much, please.'

The trusted prisoner came back with his flask. He poured coffee into a flimsy red plastic beaker. The beaker's rim was burned where a cigarette had been pressed against it. It felt rough against my lip. I tried to shrug off the conversation I'd overheard in the staff-room.

The trusted prisoner watched me as I drank. Later, I was to grow used to some of these bitter things, the taint of sweat on acrylic clothes, nicotine on breath and fingers, roll-ups smoked twelve times, the stink of coffee that some of the men said was ground from acorns.

My guide looked pleased that he'd been able to help. After he had watched me drink all the coffee, he wiped his hands down his trousers and took the beaker back to his cell. He seemed to walk with a more positive stride. I watched the flask bob at his side as he went back along the landing.

I followed him, unable to shift the bitter taste. I was afraid to look into the open doorways of cells, where men lolled on beds or sat idly munching little snacks. It's a writer's job to *look*, but in looking I felt as if I was taking the last thing that some of these men had. Instead, I trained my eyes on the suicide netting that was stretched like giant sheets of gauze between the landings.

Above us, the space was huge, a vault of stale air not unlike the rain-spoiled Methodist chapels of my youth... always these strange reminders of that other world, so close to this one, visible from the windows up here on the 3s...

On that first frightening day on the wing, a watchful, inscrutable officer gave me a safety demonstration. He showed me how to shoot the bolt in the trusted prisoner's cell. You snapped it shut, putting a bolt between the wall and the door so that no-one could lock you in.

'And this is what I do every time I visit a cell?'

'Unless you want to be held captive,' said the officer, straight-faced. 'Unless you want to find out if we think you're worth rescuing.'

Unexpectedly, his face broke into a smile full of warmth and concern. 'By hell, lad, I were only joking...'

I stared at the stiff bolt. My guide, the trusted prisoner, was staring at it too. Now there was this bolt between us and the rest of the prison. Now there was this bolt between me and him.

The bolt. I couldn't forget the bolt. It seemed proof of my fear. It seemed to confirm my lack of faith. I sat with my guide, the trusted prisoner, in his cell, playing chess. I could do whatever I wanted. I had two keys. I could go anywhere except the staff room. I had the most freedom a job has ever afforded me.

My guide beat me in four moves, a blur of motion and thought. He was a champion, he told me as he laid my King to rest. It wasn't unusual for him to have forty postal games on the go, and he expected to win them all, but he sometimes had to wait weeks for the mail to come through.

'At first they thought it was some sort of code,' he said. 'All those grids and numbers. They thought I was plotting something.'

'And were you?' I asked, an opening gambit, my first risk.

'Aye,' he said. 'I was plotting my next move.'

'So this is it,' said my boss as we approached the day's final destination. 'The Records Office. In case you want to check anything. In case you're ever worried...'

'Do *you* check?'

'I did, lad,' he said. 'Once. On my first day.'

'And you never went back?'

He didn't reply. He led me across the yard.

Near the sterile zone, along a line of wire fencing, lengths of toilet roll flared in the wind.

The Records Office was a disappointment at first sight, hundreds of manila folders inside a Portacabin that would have looked normal in an infant school playground.

But so many of them. So many envelopes, so many lives.

'Pick one,' said my boss.

'I wouldn't know where to start.'

'Start with a name you know.'

I knew only one, the name of my guide, the trusted prisoner, who had made coffee for me and beaten me in four moves.

We pulled out the file. It bulged with reports and cuttings. Testimonies in old-fashioned type. Yellowy newspapers. Faded photocopies. The trusted prisoner was older than I'd thought.

My boss remained business-like. He placed the envelope on the desk and sorted through the first few documents. Neither of us spoke. I was aware of a jet passing high over the jail, its engines here with us in the cabin. Almost as soon as I'd begun to read, I closed the folder, put it back in its rack and shut the drawer.

Neither of us spoke. We went back across the yard. I was aware of my hand and of the skin it had touched, aware now of the things that the other hand had done.

Dark shapes stood at the windows of cells and spilled their voices into the night, the only part of themselves they could free. The yard echoed with their roar, a wave always breaking.

'How do you do this job?' I asked my boss.

'You aim at the best part of a man,' he said. 'Even if you know it doesn't exist, you still aim at it.'

When it rained

They tried to pull him in that day,
but he lingered
in the yard, gulping every drop

he could get. It was summer-gear,
the rain soured by soot
and sly with town buildings,

hints of smoke and the breath
of drains, a tang of tyres
and old coats and cooling towers

and trains' brakes:
each a rumour, each a taste,
everything pouring into his hunger.

It took five men to pull him
from the fence. One screw for each
of the years since he was last wet.

Pass the parcel
For a prison yard cleaner

The cleaner pushes his barrow into the shadow
of the wing, picks up stuff other men have chucked:
Dear John notes; scooped-out oranges; the over-cooked
tea-time spuds they'd rather dump than swallow.

In yellow gloves, he'll clear the gutters of hair,
trace long strands of toilet roll along fences
to find the softest violence: shit parcels,
dense with unreadable messages.

The dead-eyed don't get it: *Volunteers*
to shovel our mess! At the skip, he tells me this:
freedom is a strange thing, you can be free in prison,
all drains lead to shining rivers.

Lost men's gifts rain into the yard — reasons
to leave his cell, walk through the wind, the sun.

First night inside

He was worn-out. Knackered.
The buzz, like. Constant.

So when he rose from the dream
in night's far quarter,

at first he lay there,
trembling worse than a dog,

no idea where he was.
And it was slow in returning:

under the light of stars,
there had been mermaids.

They'd sung beneath his window,
their gills moist with sea-water.

And he'd heard the roar
of an ocean as it drew back.

Then he had to shake himself
and climb to the bars.

'Get your tits out!'
lads were screaming

from every cell down the wing.
And, at last, he saw them:

local girls sucking Alcopops
in the street beyond the wall.

And some of them were sobbing
and some of them were singing.

And all of them more lovely
than any creature born on earth.

Sherwood

There ain't a tree for miles
but they call it a forest

'cos a forest don't need trees;
it just needs hunting.

Well, then – bang on.
They rode that one to ground.

A hundred screws on your trail
and nothing to hide behind.

Call it a forest, mate.
Call it hunting country.

Horses

Most of his stories start with horses
steaming in the pastures at dawn.

Then a female vet usually arrives
and somehow loses her clothes.

After that, gynaecological procedures
become necessary. Bright lights.

Forceps. Hooks... until I can't look.
Each week, I grope those sheets,

seeking errors to address.
What do I think? he wants to know.

Horses, I tell him. Your strength is horses.

Gone

I could have been anyone on that street,
but my luck twisted me.
The kind of loneliness I mean,
it's frightening to be near.
The gap around me widened
as the gap opened in myself.
I was like a hole inside an emptiness,
a hole something was bound to fill.
The thing I did, the blood I spilled.
She never harmed a hair on any head.
I wish someone would take
every atom from my body
and fire it at the sun.
Then I'd be good and gone.
Good and gone, mate.

Number

These things I'm sure of: fists and thunder —
learned from alleys, learned from glue.
That thing in me, it pulled me under.

Eyes of blue and golden hair —
I screamed and then I hit her. One punch, two…
two things I'm sure of: fists and thunder.

They sent me to this far place, where I'm near her,
the girl whose lips turned blue. Whose lips turned blue.
That thing in me, it pulled her under.

Dreamed it was a nightmare,
then woke to hear her ghost. Her ghost said, 'Choose
between the two: fists or thunder.'

I rolled away — I tried to shun her.
The jail rained fists, its boots made thunder — loosed
that thing which pulled me under. Under.

And now each night she sings of squander:
breath, trees, love, truth.
These things I'm sure of: fists and thunder,
that thing now me: these bones, this number.

Eye

I was doing it to myself
with my hand.
This isn't something
I want to tell you, but...

See, I realised –
this screw's eye had been
staring through the flap
for the longest time,
staring so long
I knew what it wanted.

So I get it out
from under the sheet
and shake it at the cunt.
'Go on then,' I'm shouting:
'Have a bloody good look.
This is how it works
if yours is broken!'

And the flap never wavers.
This eye there,
looking in at me
while I do it.

Yeah, sounds funny now.
But at the time, like.

The shell in the yard

I made a life on the ocean waves
Many miles from any shore
And the girl who called me home,
O, my heart to her I swore!

But a soul's at sea on dry land
When those married days turn sour
And he's washed up in the Flatlands
Many miles from any shore.

And it's true there's no excusing
What I done, and that's for sure.
Serves me right to roam this jailhouse
Many miles from any shore.

For I turned to sin and drinking
When she stretched my heart, and tore.
And I burned my boats and drifted
Many miles from any shore.

So I spend my days now sweeping
Stuff they throw on this damned floor,
The filth of prison places,
Many miles from any shore.

But today I found a sea shell
In the yard of this old jail

(Many miles from any shore
Many miles from any shore)

And I held it to my ear
And I heard the ocean's roar!

And I thought of the bird
That brought it, soaring on the air,
A beast of shining oceans,
Many miles from any shore.

And, for a moment as I held it,
I recalled the girl that I let go,
Then came back to this prison
Many miles from any shore

And I was filled with an empty feeling
For the home I'll see no more,
Another shipwreck on the waters
Many miles from any shore.

But today I found a sea shell
In the yard of this old jail

(Many miles from any shore
Many miles from any shore)

And I held it to my ear
And I heard the ocean's roar!

Cursed earth

Buggerthorpe, they called it then,
a few acres of bog on the city's rim.

You went there for a whore or a fight.
You went there if you'd fallen

through a crack in your own life.
That's where they marked out the jail's plot:

high on the moor, where all water stopped,
on earth that bloomed with thorns and gallows –

there, where men dangled for their misdeeds
and the living came in search of crimes

to ease their freedom, like the killer
who rolled dice until his victim's purse

was done, then reeled over the wilds
in search of a stream to wash his hands,

finding only the truth of a stagnant pool,
finding a woman's face in the swamp.

Godber & Miller

There was once a man called Miller,
too fat to hang.
He'd stolen cows worth a few groats
and would have swung

but the rope broke.

A Nottingham artisan called
Godber stepped out of the crowd,
said: 'I'll make you a rope.'
They would've let Miller go

till Godber showed.

The privilege of rain — Part I

I stopped him in mid flow.

'Don't say it again. Please,' I said. 'Please don't say *at the end of the day* again.'

He picked a string of skin from his thumb.

'It's a cliché,' I explained, confident in my role: I was the jail's new Writer In Residence. I had come here to help men like him with their self-expression.

Banged-up prisoners shouted from the opposite wing. Downstairs, canteen orderlies had started dishing soft-boiled potatoes onto tin plates. The air was wet with steam. Everything seemed to smell of laundry and oranges.

'And what would you know about the end of the day?' he said.

I looked at him and he seemed to smile, so I joined in, but it wasn't that kind of smile.

'At the end of the day,' he said, 'is when a stranger closes the door on you. When you hear this stranger take away the key on a chain, and the lights go out. When you start fretting whether your flask'll see you through till dawn. You're staring through the bars, trying to picture the kid you've not seen in three years, trying to remember what she looks like, her face, her eyes. Wanting to make up a nice place for her to live in, not just this dingy corner of your head. But you can't concentrate; you're on edge, waiting for something – some scream, or a bell, maybe just water in the pipes – because the guy in the next peter is addicted to flushing his toilet. And you wonder how long *this* night's going to be. Worse still – Summer. Days stretching out, on and on. Hour after hour, standing at the bars — swearing at the sky, for it to go dark. Already dreading the *next* day and the one after that...'

I fingered the keys in my pocket — two keys for the eight gates that lay between the street and me.

'So I'll ask you again,' the prisoner said softly: 'what exactly is it that you know about the end of the day, mate?'

Advice came thick and fast when I was appointed to work at HMP Nottingham: 'Don't ask what they did'... 'Prepare for frustration'... 'Sit near the door'... 'Don't raise anyone's hopes'...

But nobody warned me about the smell.

Imagine a building which has housed 130 prisoners all day, every day, for the same number of years. Imagine a place with no female scents – which smells only of men, of their food, their hair, their glands: a place where smells are sentenced to life.

Add to the sourness of the air the shrieking of kitchen tins, keys chattering on chains, the grating of chairs, banged-up men roaring. Hem the sound with razor wire, bleach it with sodium light, clothe it in nylon.

There's nowhere more real than a prison. Naturally, therefore, jails are factories of fantasy, where the lathes spark with anecdotes, jokes, tall stories, lies, denial. Prisons are a good place to send a writer. But nobody except the writer wants to be there. And the things new to the writer – the body-tastes you smuggle out – are old hat to the inmate, who dreams only of ringing a door bell, walking in a straight line, sleeping with his door open.

On my first day, in December, under a sky as pale as the prison's faces, I set three inmates to write a description of a chair. I told them to try to evoke the unmentioned person who normally sat in it.

Two of the men wrote about chairs with massive rolls of padding and pillows, chairs as places to sprawl. The other man wrote about a chair with straps and dials, and a plug.

It was my first lesson.

A lifer told me his dream. He was digging with bare hands through dry red earth.

'All this dust sifting through my fingers but I keep on digging and digging... until I start to realise – there are white bones in it, in with the dust. Hundreds and hundreds of them, very white. Tiny white bones in these handfuls of red dust, all slipping through my fingers.'

At his back, the winter moon was brilliant and low and yellow in the sky above the prison.

He stared at me. 'This dream,' he said. 'What do you think it means?'

I coughed, covered my mouth. As I started to speak, he cut me off.

'I'll tell you what I think,' he said, and he turned to point at the blazing sky. 'I think it means I've been to Mars. Either I've travelled to Mars in this life, or I was once there in a past life.'

I searched the side of his face for the joke, found nothing.

'The Red Planet,' he said, still gazing upwards.

The sky – it was always the sky.

Jets hung their trails like bunting over the prison. Wandering aimlessly, I found a gardener staring upwards. He pointed at the white trails of vapour. 'Reminds me of the 'fridge in my old house,' he said. 'Exactly the same colour of white.' He gave me some fertiliser, grey and soft, like putty, in a thin plastic bag. 'Put it on the garden at home,' he whispered, flitting his eyes to check for guards.

I lived under a flight path in a big city. That summer, blue cornflowers sprouted from the fertiliser.

Jets roared low over the garden.

A lot of the time, it was the usual stuff that a writing tutor gets used to:

'Use your *own* words, not this 18th Century language... Maybe try it without so many adjectives… Don't *think* about it – follow your pen…'

All year, I kept at it, preaching that the reader of the poem is the poet. It's in the reader's heart where the poem's action takes place. Don't crowd your reader. Don't poke her in the chest.

Some prisoners simply wanted lessons in grammar, others help writing letters. Two or three were labouring over novels. A few sought advice with legal documents.

A man with scarred hands and a wide smile wanted me to write to his girlfriend for him. 'Only it's embarrassing,' he said.

'If you're in love, that's great.'

'Okay,' he said shyly. 'Write this. Write, *Thank you for them knickers you sent.*'

I brought sonnets to my evening class, mentioned the way they bend two thirds of the way through, into a changed feeling. The men listened, fairly intent. A few of them seemed to enjoy the idea of the *volte*, the change. One of them, soft-voiced, with boxer's fists, repeated the word quietly, as if it was a taste. Two mentioned Shakespeare, how they loved his words without understanding them. We discussed the role of sound in poetry, the power of music.

All the while, prisoners shouted from behind bars on the remand wing. Unlike lifers, they were banged up in the evening, so they stood at the windows and shouted, some to their friends, others at enemies. And some called to women standing in wait beyond the walls.

Each night, as it went dark, the shouting grew louder. Tonight, something seemed to be animating the shouters more than usual, but I was unable to understand. It was a general din, like Atlantic rollers. The noise sometimes scared me – the way it kept on, its capacity for growing deeper and rawer, and deepening again.

That evening, our talk veered off, the way it often did. I don't remember the *volte*. All I remember is a mention of Byron mingling with the roar of the men in the remand wing, and that roar somehow coming inside, to the classroom.

Everyone in the room had started talking at the same time.

'The Bomb. Do you know what is planned for the fall of the Bomb?' one of the men asked me, wide-eyed. He ran his fingers backwards and forwards over the table, as if there was Braille inscribed there, a message I couldn't understand.

He said, 'They will kill us. The first thing the screws will do, when the Bomb falls, is they will fire on all lifers.' His fingers halted on the table. He fixed me with brown eyes, not unkind, but wild. 'There is a cupboard in this prison with an execution gun in it,' he said. 'You didn't know that, did you? They will put us to death rather than see us escape into the radiation and fall-out.'

It was intentness I saw there on his face, as if he could smell and touch the events he foresaw. He was thinking like a writer, drawing on the senses.

'No-one will be spared,' he said. 'These are the facts. You ask your mate, the Governor. Maybe he will tell you the facts. That there are death squads waiting to put us to death.'

It was quiet in the room again, but, across the yard, in the remand wing, the roar had kept up.

I took a breath, moved on. Talked about the connection between sonnets and romance. Talked about love.

In the tea-break, no-one threw a kettle of boiling water, as I had read in bad books and heard in gossip. Nobody sliced anybody. Nobody buggered anybody. What happened is this: the men sat down and ate biscuits I'd fetched in, and drank coffee that tasted of acorns, and one man asked if I wouldn't bother with the Jammy Dodgers any more, on account of how they clogged up his fillings.

Once, near Christmas, I escorted a prisoner between wings.

'It's years,' he said, studying the stars, 'since I was outside in night air.'

Another time, a prisoner laughed at my umbrella. 'Best is when it rains during a dry summer. There's soot in it, then. You can taste the dirt. It's real, man. Why would you want to keep out something real?'

Change was coming to the prison. Two new wings were being added to the original Victorian structure. Drills shrieked and hammers clattered. Yellow-helmeted construction workers picked their way past JCBs, trucks, and piles of bricks.

Soon, remand prisoners were to be moved into the jail, and lifers allocated a separate wing.

I remembered advice I'd been given on my first day: 'Don't change anything too quickly. In jail, change is a threat. Go easy.'

He had shot two people. In prison, they taught him to read and write, and he was angry at how the Newspapers were describing him. 'They callin me a Gangsta,' he said. 'I's a pimp, but I ain't no Gangsta.'

He wept when he told me his murders — two by-standers shot dead in a fight over drugs and girls. 'I didn't mean for that to happen, man...'

I tried to get him to see Chekhov's law: a gun in the first act always goes off in the third. 'If you hadn't taken a gun to town, it would never have happened.'

He looked stumped.

He told me about his childhood in the Caribbean, going into the hills to hunt for land crabs. They were delicacies for tourists. But the hills were full of terrors: snakes in the prickly undergrowth, and dark nights, and the Rolling Calf, a feared ghost — half man, half beast — that made a noise like a rattling chain, coming close.

On one of these trips into the hills, a young friend burned himself to death on a makeshift lamp.

When I pressed the prisoner to tell me more about the incident, he shrugged. Next day, I took him a print-out of his hunting stories. He stared at the paper with wonder. He had small hands, and held a pen gently. He was well-liked in the prison.

I found myself thinking about my Grandad. How he opened Christmas presents with a knife, and always folded up the wrapping paper to save for next year.

At Christmas, as I prepared to steal away, the jail became quieter. I asked a lifer about this. I said I'd expected trouble.

'Think about it,' he said. 'You miss family, you've got no family, you feel jealous of blokes missing families — it's all the same: you just need time to think. In the end, you want what everybody wants: you want a quiet life.'

Down at the end of the wing, two prisoners were carefully threading glittering gold and silver streamers through the suicide netting.

Soured

I'd hoped the sweets might stir memories
useful for writing. And they did. But the class
failed: 'Our childhood days, we'd prefer
to erase. Those were times to forget, sir.'

Trust

For years, the boy came home
to a silent house, his father nowhere
in sight, gone to places
they could only guess –
pubs, bookies, fancy women...

It took them years to know the rest:
that, only a few yards
above their heads
an ear had been pressed
to the attic floor, listening
to every word they said.

Month after month,
he lived in darkness and dust,
coming down only when
his sons and daughters were gone,
boiling up pots of tea,
buttering slices of bread,
then returning to the torment
of his hunt.

What did they say about him
when they thought him gone?
Was there anyone in the world
you could trust?

Prison workshop

He was up to his knees in tiny houses,
proudly swinging back walls
to show me little rooms,

everything sawed and planed
with his own hand,
dabs of grease for a stiff hinge.

'An innocent man!' he said –
'And this is how I spend my days.
Building these for a good cause.'

He stared at his chisel
as if he'd no idea what it was,
then lifted a doll by its head

and set it gently with the others
around a dining table
before washing his hands in a dark basin

until the guard motioned him
to follow across the yard
and he went back to that other box,

where no family eats in peace
and a careful hand never reaches in
to pick you up and put you back.

Bunker

After 12 months it had always been this way:
a life of pickings from market stalls,
of apples pocketed when no-one was looking

— and no-one was looking. He was nameless,
living in a concrete box on the edge
of the moor, which first smelled of piss

and later of rotten fruit, of cores tossed
to the corners and forgotten, just as he was,
a ghost in a bunker from an old war.

This is what can happen, he said, if you've fled
your dad's hands and your mother's death.
It can happen that you forget your own strangeness,

accept the fox's life as your life – become a rumour
on the skyline, where wind moves in the grass
and only the broken walls have heard of you

until you're not much more than an eye
at dawn, bagging meat when the butcher's back
is turned – raw specks good and moist in your mouth

as you skirt the dirty market's hem, watching
crates get born from trucks, draymen rolling
barrels into dark places – a new thrill

of hops and yeast in your nose, your chest –
wondering: with some of *that* in a boy,
would he really be gone – would his mind grow

as dark as the hole where he spent his days,
where he looked out on himself as if from a slit,
as if the war was coming, but he was safe.

Another country

The first travelling you ever did
was in the back of a prison van,
sent from your own country
into that new one, where the light was different.

Trev, the tall kid, masked his fright
with boasts and taunts
caught in the throat, and stopped,
and motorway concrete bumped

as you stared at miracles:
mud, puddles, kerbstones, dogs,
while Dai's fear spread through the van,
his words in all your heads:

'We'll never see Wales again',
and Trev told Dai
he'd better shut his fucking mouth,
and all the time you went further south.

How to avoid a riot

Here's what I heard: it was hot,
the whole joint bubbling
as if the lid might pop.
And the screws ready
for when it goes off.
But No. 1 stays cool,
picks up his phone,
dials the number,
says: Enough cornets
for two hundred fellas.
Plus, flakes.
And don't forget ripple –
they like blood.
One last thing –
make sure you play your tune.
Then he tells the screws:
Right, bring 'em out
in groups of ten
and any bastard
don't say please,
send him back,
make him wait.
So the men queue
with the coins they've given 'em
and the van drives in,
warbling Greensleeves
through the yard,
and they all say please,
every single one of 'em.

Dread

Hour on hour,
he waited for the abuser's feet,
for light to fill the door's crack.

It wasn't an excuse, just his story,
offered with a shrug.

Did I understand how it felt
before the door opened?
That was the worst time,
he said – before it happened,

when the harm of those other times
visited him in the quietness

and the dread reached out
like some awful hand
into the moment it had waited for,

so that he dreaded it happening
even while it happened
and was already waiting

for the next time
this time. Next time.

There are monsters who make monsters,
whose revenge is more monsters,
who are lonely,
who creep to doors,
who are monsters,
who are lonely,
who creep to doors,
who are monsters.

Said in an evening class

He says he's worked it out, this writing game:
'The reader's free; don't shut the door on him.'

A lifer offers me a cup of tea

It isn't just the burnt edges
of the plastic cup he offers,

or rumours of doctored drinks,
nor even the hands that reach to mine –

what they've become,
as spoiled and yellow as his beaker –

just the thought of fingers, once,
when he was small,

before anyone had yet
to turn away his gifts.

Passage

On that first journey home,
overhead wires reach down

to grab the train
and everything greets me as a sign.

Poles on the city's edge
have waded into power station pools,

carrying warnings on their shoulders:
DANGER. QUICKSAND.

I watch towers breathe the Trent
back in Nottingham's face

and think about that.
Ordinary things are different now:

tubes of carpet laid like corpses
under trees, pylons marching away

in chains. Miles of fencing
along the iron way.

Slowly, the towers become pots on a table,
then dwindle into their own steam.

Later, I'll reach a door
and stare down a passage

before wading back to shore,
calling: 'Only me, love. Home.'

The privilege of rain — Part II

My writing career was going badly, I had little money. After New Year, I booked into a city centre boarding house, the cheapest I could find. My room was painted mauve, with a red lampshade and a bright bulb. The television was tied by a chain to a metal shelf too high up the wall. The bed's mattress was sealed with a plastic sheet. I woke up in the middle of the night, sweating. Next door, there were loud banging noises, then silence.

Breakfast was a lump of colourless scrambled eggs, too hot, then suddenly cold. I paid up fast and walked to the prison. It was Thursday. It rained every Thursday in Nottingham. My shoes leaked.

At the bottom of the hill was a vast bakery. The street smelled of bread, and something fruity, maybe currants. All the way up the hill, smelling this dough and yeast, watching vans go in and out, seeing flashes of white-capped workers, who reminded me of the orderlies in the prison kitchen, I worried about that smell.

Would you get tired of it? Was it possible in this world even to grow sickened by the smell of bread?

An ex-squaddie told me about the guy he'd killed while on active service abroad. 'A maniac. He came at us, howling, swinging a blade. There was nothing else for it, the two of us stiffed him. I felt the blood on my hands, he was brown bread. He was brown bread, mate.'

At the end of the man's bed, two joy-riders swapped bottles of hooch. One of the men farted. They giggled, pleased with their system. The bottles were lassoed with little ropes so that they could be suspended from the bars on the outside wall if unexpected visitors popped in.

The ex-squaddie looked at his hands. He spoke very quietly. 'Later, when I reported what we'd done, the officer was furious. 'You mean you've come here to tell me you stiffed a Chink?' he said. 'Ought to have tipped him in the briny,' he told us. It was the paperwork, see. The paperwork we'd put him to.'

'Who?'

'The Writer In Residence,' I said, ashamed.

'In where?'

'Residence.'

'So you live here, do you?'

'I just teach,' I said. 'I teach people to write.'

'Fiction? Fiction's a lie. Have you come in here to teach us how to lie?'

Inside the prison, there was an old swimming pool, overlooked by the squinting windows of the Segregation Unit. Officers had pinned a sign to the wall: 'NO RUNNING OR ROUGH PLAY'. At one end of the pool was a statue of Buddha.

The pool was no longer in use. Men often stood at the bars of the Segregation Unit and stared at its dark water. Rumours said that the pool was kept on as a reservoir for putting out fires.

In April, ducks flew in to rear their young. But it was a bad spring. As I left the jail one night, I saw ducklings struggling on the tips of huge brown waves.

They didn't make it. Grown men with long criminal records wept. The mother duck wandered through the prison flower beds.

A few days later, RSPCA workers came in, and a group of prisoners helped them to fit a ramp to the pool. The ducks hatched another batch of young, which survived, and then flew away again into the vast flat places of Eastern England.

One man told me he was looking forward to their return.

The prisoner said that he had spent most of his life seeking out cliff-tops, fields, botheys, the hems of trees. He described his love of storms and camp fires. I imagined his face lit up by the flames, and the darkness of the wilderness on his back.

'I remember the smoke off the peat,' he said. 'I used to breathe in big draughts of it. It smelt like whisky.'

He told me about dancing to fiddles in an old hut, told me this as he picked boiled potatoes out of a slot in a tin plate, lights blazing in the yard.

The nights were shrinking, the world growing bigger again.

The joker stared out into the city. 'I hate this time of the year,' he said.

I looked at him.

He said, 'You remember what's out there. You can't hide from it anymore, it's there facing you.'

I was finding out about my freedom. I talked (on landings, in libraries, a greenhouse, the gym) to men with chests twice the size of mine but legs far skinnier. It was like stalking a giant galleon that was forever cresting the hill, its decks laced with wire nets, sails never rigged, the crew within sight of a port which was always out of reach.

I found a library book called *Great Walks* which hadn't been borrowed for five years.

Staff talked about 'going on the wing'; time was 'bird'. They named it 'stir', and it never moved. Cells were 'pads', as if they'd cushion a fall, or patch a wound, or launch them.

I had come 'inside' and found the edge.

Burn was what everybody wanted.

'You go mad without 'baccy,' a man explained. 'Blokes in here'll smoke anything. 'S why bananas are banned. They used to dry the skins and smoke

them. Mellow yellow. Tweet tweet tweet.'
'What's the weirdest thing you ever smoked?'
'Hair.'
'Did you feel anything?'
'Only the roots, when I pulled it out.'

In Robin Hood country, with the outlaws, my thoughts often turned to the handful of trees that had taken root in the prison. They were cut off from Sherwood by a wall, beyond which there was no longer a forest.

One of the trees, a weakly sapling, was close to the 'topping shed', where men had once been executed. I never found out what kind of tree it was, although one of the men referred to it as a sickly ash. Some men said there were bodies at its base.

'Even after they'd been killed, they couldn't escape.'

My favourite tree was the cherry blossom in the main yard. In spring, it burst into flower, dark branches sagging under the new weight.

'The last curvy thing in this whole place,' sighed a colleague.

I told him the last lines of my favourite poem, 'A Blessing' by James Wright, in which the poet suddenly realises that if he breaks out of his body, he'll burst into blossom.

Later, they drove a giant metal pole into the earth beside the tree. Workers mounted a camera on the top of it.

'Rape,' the men called it.

Afterwards, nobody knew what had triggered it. Some said it was dust in the custard, others a change in the visits regime. In one way or another, everyone blamed the prison's re-building programme, which had transformed the routines that men despised, and relied upon.

Whatever the cause, plates went flying and punches were thrown. The Governor ordered everyone to their cells. All work and education was cancelled. The men went to their windows, and roared.

The cherry tree was in wild bloom. At a loose end, I stood in the yard and gossiped with my boss. Without anyone to sweep up, blossom had pooled in pink drifts against the inside of the wall. Nearby, workers were fiddling with the drains. I watched them work, thinking about that other world below, where men's hair and skin floated free, into the sewers, to the sea.

It brought to mind the yard cleaner who willingly picked up shit parcels thrown from cells, just so that he could feel the wind on his face.

'Look,' said my boss, suddenly.

The workers had unrolled hoses.

'They're sorting out water cannons,' he said.

It was a beautiful day, warm breeze, blue sky – the type of day on which you know the world will end.

We sloped back to the Education Block, and waited.

A long time later, word came down that one of the men wanted to talk to us about his A' level in English.

We went to the yard and stood in that incoming wave of shouts, trying to get the prisoner's attention.

'Thank God,' he exclaimed when, finally, he saw us. 'I've been trying to swot up, but it's bloody impossible with all this noise. I can't think straight.'

The roar grew louder, some of it directed at us.

'But I was wondering —' he shouted, 'I was wondering – the ghost in *Hamlet*, do you think he's an actual ghost? Not that I believe in ghosts, and that. But do you think Shakespeare meant him to be more than just a symbol of guilt?'

I don't remember what I said. I probably fumbled it. I just remember hearing someone call me a bastard, and two men begging for pens. And dark smudges behind the bars, asking questions I couldn't answer.

Somewhere under the roar, a desperate man was shouting, 'Margaret!'

'What?'

His call came again: 'Margaret!'

I stood in the dark prison yard, listening.

'What?'

'Margaret!'

'What?'

'Margaret!'

He must have been standing at the bars, the woman somewhere beyond the wall. Like them, I could see nothing. All that remained of them was their grief.

'Margaret!'

'What?'

They were still calling to each other as I came out through eight gates, into the street.

'Margaret!'

'What?'

And as I climbed onto the bus back to my boarding house...

'Margaret!'

'What?'

'Margaret...'

Later, when things were calmer, I found one of the prisoners staring through the bars of the new wing, into the street beyond. He was a small man with a quiet grin, and I felt he had been badly led in life. 'Seen something you like?'

'My house.'

I laughed. 'Got your eye on a bit of property, eh?'

He nodded.

'Don't you think you should try to find a place somewhere further away?'

'Y' what?'

'When you get out,' I said. 'A clean break, sort of. Leave this place behind.'

'Why would I want to do that?'

'Well, when you're free, you can live anywhere.'

'You're not right bright for a Writer in Residence, are you? That one with the blue door. That's my house. I live there.'

We stared through the bars.

'Your house,' I said.

He looked at me like I was the world's most stupid man. 'I should have straightened the curtains,' he said.

In the new lifers' wing, one of the men proudly showed me his view. 'I can see the whole of Nottingham,' he beamed.

I didn't tell him what a forbidden map would show – that the city he'd lived in for years lay in the other direction, and his view was of drab outer suburbs.

Days later, he was still staring in wonder through the bars.

I wondered where his grey eyes had taken him – down which streets? Into whose arms? In which Nottingham?

On holiday, in Wales, a summer storm swept the cliff tops. We took cover under an ancient stone and chewed sandwiches, watching a fox forage for seagull's eggs in the rocks.

Later, in a churchyard, we put our hands on a row of yew trees that bled red sap, and then walked down a valley where we heard the locals still observed the Julian Calendar.

Finally, tired out, we crested the shoulder of a wild moor and caught sight of our cottage in the safety of the valley, far from the sharp blue stones of the Preseli Mountains, stones which the ancients had quarried for their star-temple at Stonehenge.

Back in prison, I listened to where the rumours said I'd been. I wore my tan skin furtively, like something stolen. I was full of secrets: of ocean and stars, and ancient calendars, and the trembling red fur of a fox.

A disabled prisoner had punched a governor and been carted off to the Segregation Unit. The likelihood was that he'd be 'ghosted' – spirited away to another jail.

In the weeks before throwing his punch, the man had been writing vividly about dark periods in his life, but the circles were darkening under his eyes, and his smile had lost its spark. I went down to the Seg, full of foreboding.

His bare cell overlooked the prison swimming pool. He was stripped to the waist. His only furniture was a mattress and a cardboard chair. I noticed

[57]

the delicacy of his shoulder blades, the whiteness of his thin arms.

A smile blared from his face. 'I fucking socked him one,' he said. His hands moved like wings as he told me the story. I'd never seen a man more joyous.

As I left the Segregation Unit, I was struck by its high ceilings, and tall windows, and the late summer light that flooded the building.

Grace, was the word in my head.

On Guy Fawkes Night, the loop of the year almost complete, I dragged a bag of paper and pens from my evening class, and hurried away to the staff room.

The prison's *sterile area*, a zone of high security, where no-one was allowed to venture, winked with tiny fires – rockets and Catherine wheels burning out in the dark places beneath the wire fence.

The prison was quiet. For once, there was no-one at the bars, no-one yelling. The only sounds came from the bonfire-builders on the other side of the wall. Every day, after dark, the jail's neighbours had no choice but to endure the roar of the prisoners. Now, on this one night of the year, they had licence to send fireworks pluming into the yard. Their missiles fizzed off the fences and spun in daft circles over the asphalt.

They were giddy with revenge, laughing and shouting in the manner they'd learned. All evening they went on with it, firing their rockets into the centre of our silence.

When I described the fox I'd seen on the cliff tops in Wales, I was told to open my eyes. 'There's a fox comes *here*,' the prisoner said. 'Watch for him at dawn, you'll see him. He slips out from under the Education Block.'

Two other men verified the story: 'They built this place across the line of his ancestors' paths. These bastards couldn't keep him out even if they tried. Not with the biggest fence in the world'

One man said he had seen the fox with a pigeon in its mouth. 'Like it was grinning,' he said.

That made them whoop.

Foxes and ducks. Wild, resourceful creatures living on their own terms, inside the walls.

The prisoner who was close to the end of his sentence had gate fever. Time had slowed down, he couldn't see any end to his sentence.

'I dreamed I got out, and the outside was just the same as the inside. Jesus Christ, I was hammering on the gates to get back in!'

His friend still had a year to go. He shook his head. 'No,' he said. 'Get to them gates, and, me – I'm dust.'

I told him that was a beautiful image. He only shrugged.

I arrived at HMP Nottingham shocked at how prison flattens the senses: the giant metal pole of a security camera disrupting a blossom tree's curves, the filling-in of the swimming pool with trash and a blameless tree. I had some heroic mission to use poetry to reawaken the senses of men denied colour and flavour.

I left the jail on a bus, happy to hand silver coins to a stranger who bore me no malice. From a moving window, I saw the everyday miracle of a cat. Gutters glittered with rain. I had a key in my pocket.

It occurred to me, as I looked back one last time, that I was seeing inside from the outside – from the same place that prison had allowed me to view my own life.

Seed

My deeds,
they were out of my hands.

If it's blame you want,
blame the wind.

Some lives are like that:
Seeds on the breeze, chief.

And this is the desert I landed in.
And you say I can grow here.

Sap

Not like this

Today, on the first morning of spring,
when I wanted to think of mountains,
three men told me their murders,
the first a stabbing on stairs,
the second a shotgun in the street.
I can't remember the third
 – why can't I remember the third?
The staircase won't get out of my head:
a spindly banister, skin rugs.
He broke apart when he told his story,
his sobs bunched together, hard as fists.
I call home to forget two murders
and remember the third. It's engaged,
the box smells. In my hand,
the cord is cold, slimy.
I go to the worst café I can find
and eat a mound of fried food.
No-one else is there. Curtains trail the sills
like dying seaweed. The furniture's slashed,
joined together again with black tape.
A cup sits in its own puddle.
Grit in the Formica.
A clock ticks.
This is what it's like, I think,
this is almost what it's like.

Acorns from the forest

One of my duties was coordinating the prison magazine, which was produced on old battered Amstrads in a shed near the gym. I liked this quiet job, particularly for its collaborative element, working together with a small team of men to turn out a publication that seemed to be enjoyed in the jail.

The magazine gave writers the small thrill of seeing their work in print, and provided tangible evidence of our work together.

Sometimes I worried whether the men's stories and poems, many saturated with longing and regret, might leave the writers open to ridicule or abuse. But, as time went on and inmates continued to submit their writing, I learned to relax.

A mistake, of course. Despite what tabloid columnists may say, prison is no place to relax.

The editor of the magazine winced over his morning brew. He'd had a dream, he told me: 'Coffee. Real, fresh coffee.'

How long was it since he'd last drunk such a thing?

He shrugged. 'The closest I get these days is when I wake up thinking I can smell it downstairs…'

'On the bottom landing?'

'In my house. Where I live,' he said, stumbling over his words. 'Where I used to live. I mean, I wake up not knowing where I am...'

I wondered what his home had looked like before his crime had broken it into pieces. He'd told me he had lived near the sea, and had spoken with appetite of the shining waters and of the pebbles that crunched under his feet as he walked out over the vast spaces of the beach.

When I tried to picture the coffee pot sitting in his home, I imagined summer light filling a broad staircase, gleaming photos on the walls. An ordinary place, swept clean by the woman he killed.

'Most of the lads in here,' he told me – 'they ain't monsters. They're fellas like me. They made one bad mistake and they got done for it.'

These phrases hovered in my mind for months afterwards, becoming more enigmatic as time passed.

Was this an apology or an excuse?

Or a description? Or a complaint?

Just one proper cup of the stuff, he said. That was all he wanted. 'Not that I'm obsessed or nothing – but the coffee in here, I reckon they grind it from acorns. Acorns from the forest.'

We laughed together at the idea of that. It was probably an ancient prison joke, but I was new to jails and my naivety made me a good audience for jokers, whose faces sometimes lit up with surprise when they realised I was so clueless I didn't know the punch-line.

If nothing else during my time in the prison, I gave the men that: power over the final line.

But my naivety was to have more sinister outcomes, as the magazine editor discovered to his cost.

We had turned out a decent issue of the magazine and I wanted to mark our achievement. As a special treat, I made the magazine-workers fresh coffee, and invited them to the forbidden precincts of the teachers' staff room.

It took a little doing. My two keys unlocked every door in the jail except the staff room. No one quite knew why this should be, but everyone seemed to enjoy the irony: the one safe place in the prison and I had to knock to get in.

The staff room had recently been successfully squatted by the teachers after the rebuilding programme claimed the shed which had been their previous home. It was a long, low, spacious room, as dark as a stable, and guarded by a grey metal gate. The teachers had decorated its walls with beautiful photographs of Hebredian islands, impossible white beaches backed by rugged moors and peaks. At lunchtimes, I would often stare at the pictures, wondering why we didn't all live in places like that.

The photographs haunted me when I went back to the wing. Life would be unbearable without such places. Without ocean waves and green turf.

I wondered how anyone could be denied these things and go on living.

The men perched on the staffroom chairs, gazing somewhat furtively around the staffroom, their postures stiff and awkward. Occasionally, they made twitchy looks at the door, as if expecting it to open. When I tried to get down to business, offering praise for the last issue and suggesting ideas for the next, there was little response beyond a few grunts and self-conscious nods.

As I droned on, I gained a strong impression that someone in the room hated me. I had no proof that this was true, for outwardly the men's facial expressions were as rigid as their limbs. But, on a lifers' wing, where men are denied so much information, every tiny act is given a meaning, as are the gaps and absences between acts and speech.

Silence ringing in my ears, I poured out coffee, hoping that its taste would alter the atmosphere. The men gulped it down without a word, even the magazine editor, who looked not just pale and guarded, but also somehow smaller, in these new surroundings. There was no trace of enjoyment on his face, and he never asked for a refill.

Realising that I had followed his eyes to the pictures of the Scottish islands, he dropped his gaze, as if caught in the act of a small crime. When I tried to reassure him with a smile, I offered, instead, a twitch.

'So a very g-good issue, lads,' I stammered. 'But let's make the next one even better b-b-y…'

We sat in the coffee's stink, surrounded by beautiful pictures. I realised that I was bolt-upright in the chair, copying the postures of the men. Slowly, it began to dawn on me that the chairs, a few of which had been scavenged from rubbish-skips, were probably the most comfortable seats that some of the men had sat in for years.

Through their silence, the men had spoken.

In offering them comforts, I had described their woes.

No wonder the magazine workers were suspicious of my intentions. No wonder my amiable little coffee morning was doomed to end badly.

It came with the suddenness of a playground punching.

I remembered the sensation from school: you'd finally found the courage to stare down your tormentor, and were excitedly congratulating yourself on your bravery, when, without any knowledge of it happening, you were already lying damaged in the gravel, staring up at the bully's fists.

Four guards had appeared at the staffroom's grey gate, filling the doorway with their shadows.

'Ok, lads,' said the gaffer. 'You know the score.' He spoke like a man who had seen enough and yet knew that he would see a lot more. His voice was a low growl in his throat, and barely troubled his lips.

I couldn't take my eyes from the guards' hands. They had come kitted out in see-through plastic gloves, one of them still peeling the garment over his fingers, a little slower in his preparations than the others, like a teenager fumbling with a condom. He was the one I watched while the boss spoke, something in his self-consciousness that interested me, a hesitance that gave me a little hope.

The prisoners stood up, as weary in their movements as the guard sounded when he spoke.

I watched the self-conscious officer. He was looking at the coffee pot in something like amazement.

Then I knew what they had come for.

'The *coffee!*' I blurted. 'I'm sorry, but it was my idea. I made it as a reward for…'

The chief guard kept his eyes on the men. 'You all know why we're here. No need for a fuss.'

It was a shock to be ignored with such a lack of guile. I would have preferred it if the officer had meant something by ignoring me; it would have implied that I was worthy of neglect.

The men were marched out, offering various expressions as they trooped away.

The coffee burned in my throat. I knew how it looked — as if I'd assembled the prisoners there with arrest in mind. On two of the faces, I saw weary resignation, and on another anger. It was the fourth face that bothered me: the face of the magazine editor. There was no sign of what the man was thinking, just this silent scrutiny of my face, as if he was searching me for an apology or a confession.

Or a description. Or a complaint.

I was told by an inmate that there something worse than a shark. There was the moment when you saw the parting of the water, and waited for the fin. The moment when you imagined the shark.

He told me that, for many men, this was the experience of jail: they spent hour after hour watching the water, expecting a fin.

'Sometimes I wake up in the middle of the night, knowing that somebody's about to scream. And I just lie there waiting for it, man.'

He said that, when it finally appeared, the shark was nothing. 'The shark's a relief, man. The shark's a fucking relief.'

I thought of this when I remembered the magazine staff perching on the staffroom chairs, as if wired for trouble, and wise to my tricks.

A hundred miles away in my home, I dwelled on the eyes of the young officer who had stared at the coffee pot. Still unsure why the men had been taken away, and worried that I was now a Judas figure in the jail, I rang the education department.

I was informed that the men were probably down in the Segregation Unit, standard practice in any security breach.

Security: no. 1. A mantra I had grown used to. In prison everything was secondary to good order and discipline.

'But it was just a bit of coffee… why would they punish them for drinking coffee?'

My colleague seemed not to understand what I was talking about. 'Coffee?' he said.

'As a reward…'

'I wouldn't know anything about coffee,' he said. 'The version of the story I heard, it was acrostics.'

I stared at the telephone, thinking of all the distances between us, the line out of London through the deserts of Northampton and Loughborough, the vast cooling towers on the Trent and the Lakes of Attenborough beyond. Every time I passed those pocket sized bodies of water on the train up to the prison, I looked for the sign that said: DANGER! QUICKSAND! There was something strangely reassuring about that sign; it put me on my guard when I approached, and allowed a measure of relief when I left.

My colleague in the education department spoke just a touch too cheerily. 'So I don't reckon it's coffee, lad. I reckon they've been using that magazine of yours to settle a few scores. See, if you go down through the first letter of each line, it's supposed to spell out names.'

'Whose names?'

The line crackled. 'The names of lads they reckon need teaching a lesson.'

'Ok,' I said. 'Acrostics…'

'The version I heard,' he said.

Afterwards, still not quite sure whether I'd heard my colleague right, going through the magazine backwards and forwards, I experienced a dizziness I'd previously known only as a teenager, playing LPs backwards to hear the devil's voice.

All the words I'd helped to create, all those meanings that had escaped me...

It ended, as so much prison life does, in anti-climax and disappointment. Although the magazine staff were cooler towards me in future, none seemed to blame me for his spell in the Seg. On the contrary, my involvement in the arrests seemed to have clarified matters.

The confusions of real coffee were behind us now.

The magazine editor told me that the guards had been conscientious in their duties. He said that the rubber gloves had been put to vigorous use.

'But I thought it was acrostics,' I said. 'They said it was acrostics...'

He scratched his head.

'So why did they search you?' I said. 'If it was something to do with the magazine, what could it have been? What were they looking for?'

'They don't need any reason.'

'But there must have been something...'

'Probably they were hoping, if they shook me hard enough, some words might fall out...'

Later, when I asked one of the guards what he'd been hoping to find when he searched the magazine staff, he said, 'That's a loaded question lad' and turned away.

Sap

Buds on the cherry tree
and blue sky beyond.

The sap is rising,
and men dying back.

'Summer's our winter,'
says the prisoner

who dreads blossom,
the world expanding

as he narrows,
everything he lacks

blazing from those limbs.
He stares out, and laughs:

'So that's me now.
Giving trees The Evil.'

Denial

Her murderer says he was gone when he.
When she. When the incident happened.
And he stares into the yard,
into the cherry blossom,

lately skewered with a camera pole.
Gone, too, while he does this,
while I stare after him into the boughs,
trying to imagine the moment

he's fled. 'Eyes everywhere,'
he says, far off. 'Even in that poor tree.'
Now, years on, I recall the look
that took him when the words failed.

Injustice wherever he looked,
a blameless man in jail.
He had been miles away when he.
When she. When the incident happened.

Prison visit

A long afternoon,
watching wind in the high trees.
Maybe she won't come.

I am going out with the rubbish

He'd stared out of the window
of his cell so long, he sometimes thought
the yard was his, half-expected his kids
to toddle over the sterile zone.

He wasn't cracked, though. Not yet.
So the shiny posters had turned yellow
and his paperbacks were fat with damp?
So what? He'd no time for birds
or books; he'd to keep watch.
Times in, times out. Think of the prison
as a body and the gate its mouth.
Everything needs to eat, pal.

He tapped a fist off his watch and pointed
into the yard. The bin wagon left
and the gate shut, and he said:
I'm going out with the rubbish.

Solitary

His sanity was saved by the button
he threw after lights-out
into the darkness of his cell.

It had fallen off a nylon shirt,
was nothing special, silvery-white,
stamped with four small holes for thread –

but he spent hours searching for it
on his hands and knees in the far corners,
running fingers along sill and bed.

The triumph when he found it!
Those happy moments when life
seemed to brim with purpose!

Until the bad episode
when he laid his hand on the button
and felled his chair in excitement

and the screw burst in, expecting trouble,
to find him restoring order,
muttering apologies under his breath,

the button clamped under his tongue
behind the gate of his teeth.
For if they took away his treasure

and left him alone in that bare cell
with its cardboard chair and table,
there'd be no way to go on.

From the body of a woman
For Karen Stevens

When the visiting writer asked
what they were in the mood for,
some of the prisoners giggled

and she did too.
But there was silence in the classroom
when she read their work aloud.

And some of the men laid
their faces on their arms and closed
their eyes, and I did too,

and a vision came to me
of an afternoon long ago
when our teacher read a tale of snow

and it was warm in the class,
and safe, and she was only a little angry
when she had to shake me.

Child, she said. Come on now,
child. Awake. And I came back
from wherever I'd been

to find a world
brimming under the windows
and her tune on my lips.

A bit of fluff

He'd sussed me from the off:
'You ain't a wanker
like the screws are wankers,
it ain't that. You don't want to change us,
you want to change yourself.
I bet you were bullied at school
and never got over it.
I bet someone like me did it,
someone you think was like me.

'And now you want to make the world better
for mard-arses like you.
Well, maybe you're right,
maybe you can.
But the girl I killed
will still be dead
when I get out. And dead
when I'm dead. And dead
when you're dead.
And no fucker can change that.

'So you tell your bird what I said
next time you dine out on the jail.
And make sure you talk loud enough
for the blonde on the next table,
the one you clocked when you came in,
the one you raised your game for.
Don't get me wrong, mate –
you like a bit of fluff,
who can blame you.
Who can blame you.'

Chip

The biggest sap in the whole jail.
When they flicked chips

through the netting,
one landed on his shoulder

and stuck there,
and he didn't even notice,

he was that thick,
just strutted with his tray

to the pool table
while the lads on the wing

followed after him,
shouting,

'Now you've got one
on both shoulders!'

After the reading

She wants anger, not sadness –
so I return through the wreckage
in search, stopping on the landing
where I watched a howling con
hurl oranges across the jail,
and stared into the black hole
of his mouth,

                     where hosts of memories now stirred:
                     lunchtime kickings
                     and threats behind the school.
                     A pusher with his knife.
                     And men who ran like bulls
                     through the alley in Coventry
                     where we cowered in bin-holes
                     till their rage had passed
                     while a crippled fan howled
                     from where they'd left him,
                     the wheel of his upturned chair
                     spinning

me back again to that moment
on the landing when particles of sap
spunked in the corner of my eye,
and I felt it harden in my fists:
this anger she had wanted.
As if the air parts for its virus,
And all things melt for its kiss.

Prison ballad of the prison ballad

X came to a walled-in place
Where men craved earth and sky.
He saw the wire, he saw the bars,
And he began to cry:

'O, Ma, I've travelled much too far,
too far for you to come.
I've turned my back on earth and sky,
My wandering days are done.'

They locked the door on that poor wretch
And then they doused his light
And X stood at the bars and cursed
The brilliant glare of night.

And night came on, and it was long,
Stretched out beyond the dawn,
But if it seemed long to our boy X
Think how endless for his Mum.

She was sick and frail, on waiting lists,
And came down on the bus,
And as she tottered through the yard
He listened and heard her stick –

But chose to stay in bed that day,
never showed for her Visit.
And X gazed over the yard and thought,
Not of things he'd lost,

Of earth and sky, his girl, and more,
But dates he had to cross,
The calendar where he lived his life,
As slow as grass. As moss.

Then night, and shame, fell slow and vast
And pinned him to his bunk
Till he was alone in that dark place
Where the desperate scream for junk.

And he covered his ears and howled to the bars
And spilled his voice like ink:
'O, Ma, these veins are all that's left,
They bring me drugs' bright glow

And I have found a place to live,
A shelter from this woe.'
But Ma had lost her voice by now.
It was her ghost that answered next:

'O, Son, this is your Ma to say
they laid me down to rest.
The home you left is up for sale,
Now wandering's all that's left.'

Then X went to his lonely bed
With a needle and a pen
And he wrote the ballad of his life,
Its rhymes protecting him:

'Dear Ma, I write to your old dust.
The life we shared is gone
But I will use these words as bricks
And build a house of song.

I will use these words as bricks
And build a house of song.'

Skaghead

They laughed when he explained
his plan: to run marathons
for some good cause.
A skaghead like you?
And where are you going to run it?
He'd done the maths. 350 yards
round the footy pitch, 131 laps.
Damaged, they said,
and tapped their temples.
But the cons whose pads
overlooked the field
rose as one to bring him
across the line. And afterwards
he told me his secret:
if you've been running your whole life,
running from every bad thing you ever did,
running like the boy who ran from you
over wasteland
and never made it,
then a marathon's nothing,
a marathon's more of the same.

Exchange of views between inmate and officer

'He says he's all for it,
they should bring back
the death pen.,

and I say, OK,
if that's how he wants to play it,
if that's what he's after,

he's talking to a dead man
 – but, then, if I'm not here,
if this prison ain't here –

he's out of a job,
so where does that leave *him*:
redundant,

chattering away to no-one,
and you want to be careful,
I tell him:

they can lock you up for that.'

The first line of defence

That year, one of my back teeth slowly rotted, and started falling to pieces.

I'd decided to ignore the problem, so it shouldn't have been a surprise when a splinter of the molar landed in my hand. But I was talking to a prison officer at the time, and it struck me as inconvenient.

The officer was a fascinating man, obsessed with criminology, and keen not to be disturbed from his reading of text books. As he talked, I attempted to listen while clutching the fragment of tooth in my fist. He told me about the graphs that had finally been used to catch the Yorkshire Ripper. Statisticians had marked the time of attack down the vertical axis and the place of murder along the horizontal. By plotting a line between the dots, detectives had narrowed the focus of their search to just a handful of streets.

The officer's eyes gleamed when he explained this, a joyful light released into this place of dullness and woe. Did I see how simple their method was, how beautiful?

My tongue explored the cavity. There seemed to be a hole the size of a meteorite crater. I tried not to wince. I didn't want a prison officer to see me wincing. This seemed important somehow.

'Yes,' I nodded. 'It's like good writing.'

He frowned a little.

'I mean,' I stammered, 'it's like my idea of good writing. The effects are amazing, but the thing itself is simple.'

He shook his head.

'I see,' he said.

In the interval granted by his frown, I decided to put the fragment of my tooth behind the radiator in his office. It struck me as interesting that a small part of me would always be in prison. After that, I wandered away down the wing, ruminating upon the officer's fresh-faced enthusiasm for his subject.

It was the kind of conversation that I'd been desperate to have ever since entering the jail, where the greatest mystery remained the officers. I wondered what kinds of people were attracted to this difficult job, where a simple bunch of keys gave you so much power, and so many reasons to be hated. I wanted to know how such a job affected those who tried to do it.

Most of my attempts to gain answers met with tight-lipped responses. I could understand that. As a convict once said to me: 'It's only madmen who ain't paranoid in this place. Paranoia's your first line of defence, mate.'

On my way towards the gate, glad and privileged to be putting the jail behind me for another night, I was approached by a female officer, stealthy and watchful in her movements. She asked if it was true that I was a writer.

It was a hard question to answer. If you judge someone's occupation by their earnings, then I wasn't much of a writer.

Before I could blurt out any sort of reply, she told me that *she'd* been writing quite a lot, writing in most of her spare time and she wondered if... she wondered...

Her thin lips stopped moving. I was shocked to see how nervous she'd become. Her eyes were locked on full-beam, roving across the yard, then sweeping back like lights over my face. Her gaze was unnerving. She had a compact, well-made face, but some urgent internal pressure was squeezing it shut.

Just for a moment, so intense was her scrutiny, I had the feeling that it was *me* who had the secret and *she* who was desperate to hear it. Now I understood how a blameless person could come to confess a crime they had never committed. And I saw, too, how they might thank their inquisitor for the privilege.

'If you're writing,' I said to her, 'please let me see it. Show me the...'

Few sentences ever finished. So hard to listen in a place full of eyes, in a place where every scrap of information can be used against you...

Two male officers were sauntering towards us in that strange slow-motion manner their tribe had perfected.

'Not now,' she said.

'Right,' I said.

'Later,' she mumbled.

She turned and paced towards her colleagues. Her stride was brisk and full of purpose, and she didn't break it.

There was another officer, a burly man with narrow eyes, who always seemed to be tracking my movements. While talking to prisoners, I would turn to find him watching, his gaze steady and meticulous.

The officer's eyes shone with a curious gaiety and puzzlement whenever we spoke, as if he was a bright child making his first encounter with algebra. I could never work out if he was amused by my cluelessness, or perhaps simply astonished that people in the world did jobs as ridiculous as mine.

Perhaps it was the latter. If so, that maybe explained why I enjoyed his company, even though I didn't entirely trust him. For I was similarly confused by prison guards like him.

Who were they?

Why had they *chosen* this place?

Then came the invitation.

The burly guard had told the other officers that I liked football and now they wondered whether I wanted to join them in a game. Or did I just watch?

I told them I played. I tried to make this very clear. I didn't want them to put me in one of their little boxes. I was a player.

Good, they said. The gym is free at midday when the cons are in their cells. Bring your kit and join us.

I trained for the match by running on local hills. On one of those runs, it occurred to me that the burly officer may have been *officially* assigned to track my movements.

Illegal items enter a prison in a limited number of ways. They are passed on at open visits or hidden in delivery trucks. Alternatively, they can be brought in by members of staff. That includes chaplains and doctors and writers-in-residence and prison guards and whoever else enters a jail to service its needs. I'd heard stories of bent officers, but seen nothing untoward. There were also tales of writers-in-residence who had gone off the rails.

Someone clearly brought in the men's gear. So the possibility that I was under suspicion shouldn't have surprised me.

It's only madmen who ain't paranoid in this place, mate.

It all started to make sense. The officers were going to keep me right where they could see me. Their intention was to prove that I was soft. The game would show me who I was messing with.

These were the thoughts in my head. This was the sense I made of their invitation.

I devised a strategy, learned from years of teaching: if you want to go out nice, make sure you come in nasty.

We undressed together in the gym after watching the prisoners file out. A few of the inmates nodded at me, many huge torsos, many thin legs. All of them glowed from pressing weights.

Pain is a leveller, or so a convict had told me. I kept that thought in mind as I removed my clothes, watching the guard undress.

Ten mammals hanging their stuff on hooks, shirts and trousers dangling like pelts in the murk…

The first tackle, I hit him hard. I'm not normally a dirty player, but I knew the script now.

Now they know who they're dealing with, I thought.

Now my card is marked.

My victim clutched his knee, his mouth a grey hole, the bar of a scowl down his forehead.

The oldest player, a man of 62, proud of his sporting prowess, stood with his hands on his hips. 'By hell, lad. It's nobbut a game.'

I realised they had all stopped playing, and were staring at me, including the man I'd fouled. He was getting to his feet now, and not happy.

'No sliding tackles indoors,' he glowered.

I followed his finger to the wall.

'Funny sort of writer as can't read,' he said.

Truth is, I was sick of signs.

FORBIDDEN. WARNING. ALWAYS. NEVER.

We went on with whatever game it was that we were playing. I spent the whole match expecting to be crunched into a wall bar, wondering which of the victim's colleagues would take revenge on his behalf, not quite trusting the nippy 62-year-old with the tricky feet.

When no one attacked me, and the game flowed to its enjoyable conclusion, I suffered a weird mixture of elation and disappointment. Elation at playing well. Disappointment that the officers had exceeded my expectations.

Was that part of their plan? Or *was* there no plan?

And what the hell had *my* plan been all about?

In the changing room after the game, the 62-year-old told me that he was sixty-two, at length.

Meanwhile, the burly man watched me talking.

One of the quietest of our company, whom I'd barely noticed during the game, such was the careful simplicity of his passing, had begun to fit together his uniform as if tightening screws to a boiler, each crease firmed and pressed, each cufflink a shining rivet, the tie fastened hard as a metal brace.

'Will you be coming again?' he said.

'I'd like to,' I replied, and felt the lack of urging.

'Not bad,' he said. 'You weren't even all that bad.'

'Bit of a psycho, like,' said his mate, stooping to fasten a lace, sardonic voice half-blocked by his body.

'They lock blokes up for less,' said the quiet man. 'Isn't that right, eh?' He jabbed a third man in the ribs.

This was my victim, the officer I'd fouled.

My victim said, 'Aye, but some of them deserve worse.'

Our eyes met. Mine must have been as wide as manhole covers. His tightened to slits. He didn't seem to know that he was my victim.

'What do you mean?' I said. 'That they should be locked up for longer?'

He screwed on his cap and brought it down almost as far as his eyes in a way that many of the prisoners hated. 'I mean,' he said, 'that they should lock 'em up 24/7. I mean that they should lock them up and throw away the keys.'

'That's the printable version,' his friend laughed. 'That's what he tells lads like you.'

The others joined in with the joking, but the man kept his eyes on me, as hard and shiny as little coins. I felt them on my back as I went up the slope towards the wing, and I wondered whether I'd been given a warning or some strange portion of grace.

Later, when I bumped into the female officer who had mentioned her writing, she frowned when I brought up the subject.

'Me?' she said.

'You stopped me in the yard and...'

'I don't know anything about any writing, sir. You must have the wrong person.'

She strode off across the yard to attend to another of her duties.

I stared at the cherry tree, its branches bare against Sherwood's winter. Difficult to believe that it was capable of blossom. Or that anything here could ever bear fruit.

Returning for another game the following week, I heard the whooping of alarms, and was almost swept down the slope by a platoon of officers as they rushed towards the gym. Whatever had happened in there, I wondered how they'd deal with it, this collection of the stout and the elderly and the mean and the kind-hearted. These riddles called to solve another puzzle.

In the early days of the job, I would have gone down to the gym and peered in, afraid and curious. *Fascinated*, as in that word's ancient sense: under a spell, bewitched. Now I knew what I would see: another set of blokes vibrating with various angers.

I turned and went back up the slope, staring at the wing's huge edifice. I remembered the piece of tooth behind the radiator. I wondered whether it would ever be found. Somewhere high in that building, a man would be hunkered over a book on criminology, eyes shining as he considered its simple beauties. I thought of his fate: to stand in attendance after the beast had been gored, rather than to know the thrill of the chase.

What battles did the officer face to protect his zest? Were there were people in the jail who hated his optimism and wanted to crush it?

Wherever that man is now, on whichever curve of whatever strange graph, I wish him well. I wish him streets and fields.

Seizure
pris-on, n. [F prisoun <L prahensio, -onis seizure]

Hours before,
he knows it's coming.
Knows it the way
a dog knows thunder,
in his teeth and hair.
Soon they'll lace him
with chains
and load him into a van,
take him to the ward
in the hospital
in Nottingham
where he'll spend the night
fighting the pains
that quake in his bones,
free at last of jail,
still cuffed to himself.

Craft

Words have slipped
their moorings, gone solo.
All week, he labours over
a story about a killing
then reads it to a shocked visitor,
forgetting the facts,
thinking only of craft.
'The way words escape.
How proud you get.'
How they roam the place.

The angel of old men's shins

He says the walls are the colour
of drizzle and that everything tastes
like the onset of `flu, smells
of baggy ankle socks that perverts wear.

It doesn't matter. A guardian spirit
watches over him, and has been his calm
since he first put his kit in the box
and she whispered he was safe from harm.

He's not alone. The landings are roamed
by angels, who search out blokes
afraid of going under, the ones
that can't get out of their heads

or who have gone out of their heads
staring into the yard, whose eyes
have stalled in the *sterile zone*,
where nothing moves, only orange peels

against a fence, in the breeze.
Minor angels on the wind's breath:
guardians of watered gravy, shiny carpets,
old men's shins and metered tellies.

Our Lady Of The Scratchy Curtain Runners,
of the boarding house with thin black stairs.
Angel who steams from you at first light,
from the cold bed. Who falters, slips.

It doesn't matter. When wind comes
and blows petals against the wall,
he'll keep the faith – stare at that drift
until he's part of its blossom.

Safe

I have not been touched by her hand,
nor felt it move through the drizzle
that might shine on a coat.

Not shivered as her fingers trail the arm
to the sleeve. To hover on the sleeve
and then slide into the clasp.

Not closed my own fingers
around her quiet bones, nor seen
the slow beat of those eyes,

the steady gaze which says, through rain:
'I am watching. You are safe.'
Not heard that, nor seen the mouth

which forms the kiss. But I have felt her
deep in the chalks and irons
that make me more than stone.

I have known silence and also trust.
And I have watched the slow comings
of dawn over the slates of this jail,

wondering how the days get here
and where they go. And who I am.
And how I know that I am safe.

Song of the flask

Banged-up in a pad with no power points,
a flask of hot char lasts till dawn,
but sometimes he wakes and tries to trace
the disturbance to aches
in his stomach or a far-off pipe
or the wind or a dream –
then curses the lid's dodgy thread
and the steam for escaping.

Said on a landing

Guilty men cry hardest
but the innocent cry longer.
Give them ten years:
that'll sort out who to pardon.

Bolt

I'm taught how to shoot the bolt on a cell door,
jamming the catch against kidnap. I know I must,
but it rubs salt in our wounded trust

so I lapse, leaving the bolt unshot
while visiting a man they say needs company.
He gets it. A guard locks me in with him

for the longest three minutes of my life,
a vast door shut, alone with the lonely,
and nothing good, just a bed-frame,

mustard paint, dust, deadened thuds –
until, point made, the guard opens up, tuts,
'Liked that in there, did you?' and I leave, fast.

Styx

I told the men the little I knew
of rivers: that a 'rival' is someone
who competes for water.
And that arrival means
'bring a ship to shore'.
Rivers of the Underworld, I said,
wondering if I'd travelled too far
up the course of the subject,
whether in my eagerness
to set minds free
I'd reminded the men
of where they were berthed.
But the Acheron, the Styx –
well, they earned some mirth.
Not to mention the third one,
the one they were on...
Shit Creek, as the lifer said.

A place to live
That is what language is: a habitable grief
                              Eavan Boland

That day, the jailed man built a home from things
he'd lost — dug white faces from peat, set them
to work finding stones on the moors' old reef

while he used the verb of his hands to make
the bothey's roof – oak trees stripped of bark,
later sealed with nouns – slabs of turf, soaking rain.

Soon, he'd let his ghosts in from the wind,
thank them with drink, keen to their talk.
But, for now, it was enough to lie on his back

facing the roof's last gap – to breathe in smoke
as blue as his loneliness, as blue
as the sky through a cage of branches.

Empire

Diana was dead, and it didn't much
bother me, except in the way I'd bother
over any mammal killed in a tunnel.

After all, the Royals' ancestors
had never stopped their wars
when my townsfolk were slain,

so I went on working in the days
after the crash, deflecting mournful talk
with lessons on craft and technique,

until the men's sadness made me feel unkind.
One inmate wept when he spoke of her:
England's rose, cut down in her prime.

I bit my lip and did my job, whatever
that meant, whoever I was trying to be,
and, later, when I got off the bus

and was sneaking to my lodgings, as if scared
of being seen, a smell of blossom
lured me to the town hall, where families wept

as they laid flowers on the steps
and roamed the high byres, writing notes
of distress, the ancient town as hard as ever,

its drunks still rolling through the streets,
but this fragrance at the back of things
and tattooed strangers releasing griefs.

The Spin

He's wise after his Spin:
'Five nicks in five nights,

then back where I began,

or so it would seem',
and looks at the floor

as if to check he's still on it.

Not the words
or how they're spoken,

but the silences between.

Not the chapter,
not the verse,

but the empty thing around it.

Five days in the van,
he forgot where he was

and who had forgotten:

'Like an atom, mate –
made of holes',

then turns away, his piece done.

Not the words
or how they're spoken,

but the silences between.

Not the chapter,
not the verse,

but the empty thing around it.

No need for rivers

All that year, the lifer had written eagerly. But the river stumped him. His pen wouldn't move.

'Okay – any water,' I told him. 'Call to mind the sea or a lake. Imagine you're staring upon it, or swimming. Then let go. Describe it without thinking.'

His frown deepened into a mid-ocean trench. 'But I've never seen a river,' he said.

What I recall now is the greyness of his hair, the dry nature of his skin, a man younger than me, who had lived much longer.

'The thing is,' he said – 'before I came here, I never went outside much, never needed to.'

Others in the prison writing group were nodding slowly, looking at their pencils as he spoke.

'Most of my work,' he said, 'I did indoors. The deals, the hits: indoors. It isn't like you see it in the films. *You don't flounce about.* You go where the Old Bill can't see. You drive to people's houses in the dark. And do the business. And come back out. And go to the next joint. Like that, see? All night. Over and over. In the dark, where no-one can see.'

I tried to nod wisely.

'That's what people like you don't get,' he said. 'Work like that, you need eyes in the back of your head. Because it takes up all your energy. Pressure, see. A lot of pressure. And there ain't no time for fancy day trips, mate. Nor any need for rivers.'

No need for rivers. I wanted to tell the man he'd never valued his freedom. I wanted to explain that this was also true of me, that prison was our teacher, and could perhaps somehow set us all free.

But he was still in the flow, explaining his former life, a series of rooms connected by street-lights and roads, rarely a meadow or a hill, nowt at all that would stand in the way of his purpose.

Outside, the yard echoed with the shouts of banged-up men.

'Except this one time I scored a deal in this park,' said the lifer. 'Trees everywhere. Branches and twigs and that. Creepy as fuck.'

'Probably full of criminals too,' said the joker across the desk.

The lifer rationed out a smile. 'Some park in Birmingham, I think it must have been. And don't ask me why, but I ended up by this lake or pond or whatever. And there was something in the light; I noticed the water. So I put my arm in up to here, up to the elbow, and I looked at it under the water. My own fucking arm. Just staring at it like a gobshite, how white it seemed. And the water and the light. And then this thought came in my head.'

'First time for everything,' said the joker.

'This thought,' said the dealer, hypnotised by his memory. 'I mean, they'd probably bang me up if I said it out there…'

He stared over the flat surface of the desk as if it was the vast, mystifying expanse of his mind.

'See, there was something about the water that I noticed. It looked thick, very thick. And then this thought came to me: I'm here. That was it. Nowt else. It struck me, like: how thick the water seemed. And me with my arm in it. This is me, I thought. I'm here.

'I ain't nowhere else, except here.'

Beyond the wall

In bed, after dark,
in the calm hour
before it starts again,
he prepares to leave,
packing that secret bag
where he stows
the key to eight gates.

The chain's song
is quieter
than air in a sleeve,
and he's gone
down Perry Road,
and if he turns left
he'll be on
the main drag
and all of Nottingham
will lie beyond.

Stump .

The roar

This thing inside the scream
and all around it

which dins at the back of everything.
In the roots. In the core.

The thing not heard and never spoken,
which can't be named or touched –

and which the men brim with
when they stand at the bars and roar.

The song of the goat

He wrote of the night he'd sailed out into the gulf beyond England, currents churning in the deeps of the water while the lights of home began to fade over the horizon. At the prow of the ferry, rain stung his eyes as he stared into the future, and he wondered where this new life would take him.

Of his crime, not a word.

Whatever had propelled the man to leave, I would have to guess from the clues offered by his eyes, which burned as if they were still staring into that wind.

He had introduced himself in the prison chapel, an unexpectedly roomy hall that opened like a meadow in a recess beyond the ancient wing. His hands were small, and his hand-shake gentle. Once again, I was left wondering about the other lives a man might have lived – and, also, of the life that might have been mine if my parents had separated when I was a child and I had gone looking for the wrong people to impress.

He was anxious to make me a cup of tea, and to explain himself while I drank it. The list of sorrows that he recited was hard to bear, a seemingly endless litany of illness and death, as if it were the negative image of a family tree, each of its names and combinations offered as proof of obliteration rather than the chain of life that had summoned him from dust.

As he spoke, his teeth barely parted for the words, and, although his voice remained quiet, it travelled like a fully-laden bomber, low and heavy, searching out its target with deadly intent. Here was a grief more like anger than sadness, anger that boiled in every vessel of his blood. I wondered whether I could deal with it.

When he took a pause for breath, before he could go on with his endless list, I took a risk and broke in. I told the grieving man that I could offer him only one piece of advice, and warned him that it may prove useless.

'Read,' I said.

He cocked his head, another gentle gesture at odds with the rage that throbbed in his veins.

Books, I said. Books can expand a mind, and also maybe save it. As well as company, they offer consolation and solidarity. In the company of great books, we may find that we are no longer alone. I quoted words I loved by the American novelist Cormac McCarthy, words that had helped me through my own tragedies:

'The closest bonds that we will ever know are bonds of grief, the deepest community one of sorrow.'

His gaze flickered slowly over the skin of my face, as if searching for a secret hollow that would reveal meaning or reason.

'I don't know why I told you that,' I said. 'I just thought it might help…'

The man's eyes burned. 'They let me go to her funeral,' he said. 'Yeah. But they made sure there were all these *conditions*...'

'Okay,' I said, lost in his story as surely as he was lost in grief and anger.

'Imagine it,' he said: 'standing in chains before your own mother's grave.'

In the weeks that followed, I managed to establish a working relationship with the grieving man, who had worked out very quickly that I wasn't important enough to cause trouble with or complain to.

The only power is no power. That's what it says in a great book, *Riddley Walker* by Russell Hoban. Working in the jail, I used the phrase as a mantra and a path. As soon as the inmates worked out that I occupied roughly the same place in the prison hierarchy as the Buddhist minister, they relaxed a little.

Then I could get things done.

The grieving man seemed to understand this, although there remained an aura around him that I found a little unsettling and which I was tempted to dispel by visiting the Records Office. However, having suffered misgivings over several prisoners, I had recently made a vow that I would stay away from those files, at least until my final day in the jail.

On my final day in the jail, I wasn't sure what I would do.

It turned out that the grieving man could write. Although he sometimes grew frustrated with the shapes that his words refused to take, such was his capacity for concentration, he proved capable of filling page after page, sometimes forgetting to move while he wrote, so that his fingers were blue with cold when he was done.

When he held a pen, he made a fist of his hand and gripped it like a chisel, the phrases engraved rather than written, as if carved into a gravestone. He had discovered a channel for his intensity, a channel beyond revenge and self-harm and riot. It thrilled us.

'I've found a way of doing my time,' he cried, wielding the wad of paper as triumphant proof. Each word was shouted from the page, in large capital letters. 'I can go all night,' he said. 'All night! And suddenly it's daylight and I never even noticed. The hours *burn*, mate.'

I quoted Wordsworth's recipe for powerful writing: *strong emotion, recollected in tranquillity*.

The grieving man snorted like a horse. 'Tranquillity?' he said. 'In this joint? That's a laugh.'

No matter how ridiculous he found my stolen maxims, he went on writing, the prose nagging away at the frustrations of married life and prison but occasionally yielding to fleeting moments of childhood happiness at his mother's side, a relief from his grief and anger, although less compelling.

The day he showed me his tale of leaving England by boat, I knew we were on to something.

'Where were you hoping to reach?' I asked him.

'Wherever the Legion sent me,' he said.

Soon he was so deep into his tale, there were marks on his fingers where the pen had bit into his skin. It was vivid stuff, the autobiography of a man who had fled unspecified trouble and found haven in a foreign army, where the recruits were taunted by a savage commander who strutted through the ranks, carrying a tiny, vicious monkey on his shoulder.

His prose was raw and urgent, a bayonet twisting into a wound, over and over. Each page burned with the frustrations of distance, its protagonist divided from his fellow beings by gulfs not just of geography and language but also culture and temperament.

Whenever the furious recruit was forced to drop to the dirt and perform another press-up, I went down with him. And I was there each time he came up, filthy and snarling, and covered in sweat. And I struggled with him when he tried to buckle his awkward tongue around another impossible foreign phrase.

His writing was the howl of a man who had been swept away. It was a voice that knew it may never be heard, a howl across the darkest gulf.

At home in the evenings, I corrected grammatical errors in descriptions of the parched lands where he roamed, marking the man's script with suggestions on how he could crank up suspense and improve the flow of the narrative.

'If you switch things round here and there,' I advised, 'then you'll keep the reader guessing a bit more.'

'But what if that isn't the order they happened in?'

'Who'll know?' I said.

He bit his pen. 'So you can just change things?'

'Maybe. If it makes the story work.'

'I never knew you could just change things,' he said.

It struck me that the man's absorption in his writing justified my presence in the jail, where good order and security were the major priorities. Although I sensed there were guards who hated me for disturbing the prison's routines, I suspected they had colleagues who appreciated pens more than they did bricks and shivs.

At the time, it never occurred to me that I had become complicit with a system I disliked, where education and rehabilitation were low on the list of priorities. This realisation came later, when the pride had worn off, and I was examining other delusions which had developed while I was trying to survive the jail's onslaught of ideas and odours.

All winter, we worked on drafts of his autobiography, the man's excitement warring with his frustration.

Often, he grew confused.

'I don't know which bit to write next. You need to tell me.'

I said I wouldn't know which bit came next until I saw the whole story. I advised him to think in scenes, and to forget the bigger picture. We could start patching things together when we had all the pieces.

He squeezed the pen in his fist and made as if to jab it into his bunk. 'It's getting to me,' he said.

'The book?'

'All of it. The book. These fuckers. Everything.'

'Remember what you said about writing. How it could help you to do your time.'

He looked at me, his expression blank.

'*You* told me that,' I said.

He shrugged, his body so charged with tension that I expected his neck to buckle when the shoulders crunched against it. 'They're taking the piss,' he said. 'I've warned them, but they never listen. It's going to need sorting out. I'm going to have to deck him.'

'Deck who?'

'The wing governor. He's been asking for it and I'm going to have to do it.'

'But you'll end up worse off.'

'Not after I've clocked him one, I won't.'

'Yeah, but the satisfaction will soon wear off. Then you'll be back where you started.'

He rubbed a hand over his knuckles in that gentle way of his, the pen still lodged fast in his fist.

'Look,' I said: 'next time you feel like popping someone, why don't you count to ten instead?'

He shifted his attention from his knuckles to my face. The whites of his eyes were red and bleary, but something stirred in the irises, a milky swirl that made me uneasy. 'Are you saying I can't count?' he growled.

'No, I...'

'Just because you think I'm thick, it doesn't give you the right to...'

'But I wasn't saying that.'

'I can fucking count, mate. I can count as good as you. That's all there is to do in this place: count. You count things that nobody else ever counted. I know how many bricks there are in that wall over there. The exact number. So don't tell me I can't fucking count.'

'I know you can count. Next time you feel like punching someone, do that instead. Count to ten.'

The depths of his eyes went on swirling, like water under the blades of a ferry.

'So that you give yourself a few seconds to think,' I said. 'And then you'll be able to make a proper decision...'

He put down his pen and rubbed his knuckles very gently, the fingers still curled into the loosest of fists. 'Count to ten,' he muttered. It seemed that he had lived for over forty years without considering this advice. Perhaps he had never been offered it. I wondered what he had learned when he was a child, and who had taught him. Did someone cut away his moorings? Or was he born adrift?

We both knew the fire was burning out.

A hundred pages into the book, he said he needed a break. I said I understood. He let me know by his expression that I understood nothing. 'It's your *job*,' he said. 'You should be *helping*.'

After that, I received no more pages of the autobiography.

On my final day in the prison, a prisoner took me to one side on the stairs beneath a landing. 'Look, mate, it's about time someone told you…'

'Told me what?'

'Something you should have worked out ages ago.'

I let whatever was coming continue on its path. I'd seen a handful of prisoners do that. It always impressed me. Rather than shutting it out, they threw the door open, and ushered it in.

'I'm telling you this because you don't deserve it,' said the man.

'Telling me what?'

'Because we don't think it's fair. And someone should have told you.'

'Yes. But told me *what*?'

He looked over his shoulder. 'I'll not beat about the bush. There are only two lads in this joint who've been in the Foreign Legion.'

'And?'

'And yet there are three who've told you they were.'

'Meaning?'

'Meaning you should check their knuckles, mate.'

'Whose knuckles?'

'The knuckles of them three blokes who've told you they were in the Foreign Legion.'

'Thanks,' I said.

'You're welcome.' He pretended to turn away.

'But why?' I said. '*Why* should I check their knuckles?'

The prisoner faced me. 'To find out if they were in the Legion, you dipstick. If they were in the Legion, they'll have this scar on their hand. Here.' He held up his hand to show me. 'So now you can see that I was never in the Legion.'

'Because there's no scar,' I said.

'That's what they've done, see. They've slashed their hands and joined the cuts together…'

'Blood brothers… and you can tell by the scar if they've been in the Legion…'

The prisoner did a bit of mock applause. 'Blimey, you catch on fast. Must be because you're intelligent, eh? Because you're a writer?'

'So all I've got to do…'

'… is check their hands,' he beamed, applauding a little more quietly.

I spent my last afternoon wandering around the jail, staring at hundred of hands, trying to read fortunes from every nick and scar. One man's hands were mottled with a swarm of black spots, like leaves on a tree at the back-end of summer. I was told it was the result of an attack with sugar and boiling water, a favourite ploy against paedophiles and sex offenders. The heat of the water makes the sugar stick to the skin, and the victim then carries his stigma forever.

All this skin where there had once been only leaves.

I thought of the forest that had grown here, and the legendary outlaws that had wandered its groves. After the oaks and ashes were hacked down, the earth had turned to bog, and the few remaining trees were laced with nooses. Buggerthorpe, they called it then, a waste haunted by criminals and prostitutes, in whose ruined acres even the water slowed to a crawl.

Were some places cursed to carry their scars forever? Was the poet Chris Jones right: are there men on this earth for whom life holds no love?

While I pondered the wisdom of climbing the landings so that I could stare at the hands of the grieving man, I was torn by a general indecision. It was my last day in the jail, a final opportunity to visit the Records Office. If I wanted to discover what my students had been found guilty of, this was the moment.

Something inside me burned to know.

But what would be the point of reading about those crimes? What exactly would that achieve?

Closure?

It occurred to me that I might have nightmares for years if I read the files, and that maybe I *should* have nightmares for years, since that would be better than congratulating myself on little triumphs over sonnets and syntax.

I was tired, and didn't want to stare at any more hands. The fortunes of all that sallow prison flesh frightened me. Its stories were overwhelming. On the verge of climbing to the landing of the grieving man for one final meeting, I decided to pack it in. There had been hundreds of opportunities for me to study his fingers, and I'd spurned them all. I'd had enough of trying to read the jail. Its codes were difficult to crack, and the messages hardly ever made sense.

Walking past the Records Office, still not sure whether I would go in, I set my eyes on the sky, where sodium lights bruised the backsides of clouds. It was difficult to work out what I'd achieved with the grieving man. Had I helped him to release vivid memories? Or colluded in a denial? And further damaged an unstable personality?

Fiction or fantasy, did it matter anyway? The prisoner had done his time quietly for a while.

Maybe that was enough.

On the other side of the wall, a woman was shouting to her man. Although he didn't answer, she kept on shouting. And I could still hear her voice when I was several blocks from the jail.

It was the last sound I carried out of that place, the plaintive wail of a creature parted from its mate.

I had recently heard a theory about the origin of our word, 'tragedy', and I thought of it now as I waited for the bus to take me away. Like every word in our language, 'tragedy' has crossed enormous distances of time and place. It is thought to have been born from two separate Greek words, 'song' and 'goat'. Some linguists suggest that the word refers to the separation of the kid from its mother. The creatures would call to each other across the gulf between Greek islands. Hence, the word contains, at its heart, division and yearning.

The agony of separation. I heard it now in the woman's woeful cry. And I had heard it many times in the writing of prisoners.

If the prisoner was there, he never answered.

But she went on singing from the darkness beyond the wall.

Stump

Bollocks, we invented it!
Those lads had been kicking bladders

since they were fucking ancient.
We just drew squares in the grass

and gave some wankers in black
a flag and a whistle.

The Brits love a box, man.
Look at Egypt. We drew them

their whole pitch in the sand.
Our own forests: chopped down

for squares. Aye, so lads in white
could throw pelts at spears.

So it'd make more sense
the other way round? So what?

The rules don't make no sense, mate,
and that's the sense they make.

Said on a landing

All night wondering
about life in the next world.
But where are we now?

Refused

Turned away by a minion at the gate,
the woman weeps quietly into her hands
while the toddler by her side chafes
for release and the baby in the pram
screams. She lurches for her fella's jailers
as if yanked by a chain, the protest bursting
in her throat: 'What do you mean, *papers*?'
The gateman repeats the rules. Calm. Certain.
Her eyes meet mine, a dull colour, the wrong
side of grey. 'Three buses,' she gasps: 'Three buses
from Manchester. And now this.' She flings
her young life at the pram and pushes
it hard down Sherwood Rise, her kids
famished and uneasy, her face unkissed.

Mike's girl

I told him straight,
it's either me or the weapons.
You get them weapons
out this house
or I walk.
but you know Mike,
what the fuck is he like.
I should talk to that wall.
Him with a weapon!
He can't even piss straight!
Plastic fucking gangster,
all gob and trousers.
You lose them weapons,
I shout,
or that's me. Out.
And the bastard's waving!

Ghosted

He's young and keen,
and we make progress,
but next week his seat's vacant.

I read his poem again:
To My Dad, With Love.
His mate's voice is hushed:

'Three of the choices are easy.
Break your cell. Or a con.
Or a screw.' And the fourth?

'Yourself.'
They tell me he was ghosted
to a new environment

for his own good.
And they'll be scrubbing his cell
for a while yet.

Stir

Mid-December, and,
at a quarter past four,
the day is crushed.

An ocean's light pours
from a darkened classroom –
some rare softness.

I unlock the door,
slip quietly, unnoticed, into
that deep pool.

The men are watching
dolphins on television,
razored skulls swaying,

grey faces washed blue
as they float through strange waters,
where killer whales rise

with jaws opened.
Then lights roar, and guards lead
them down a passage

whose yellow walls drool
with kitchen smoke and boilings.
But their eyes gleam.

Carnage

When he comes to my pad tomorrow –
after the Buddhist priest has slung his hook
and I've sorted that debt on the wing —

I'm going to open this plastic envelope
and ease them from their binding,
the photos I told him he must see,

the things we did at Goose Green.
For I am sick of the lot of them,
that lollypop of a therapist

who nods when I confess my sins
and her mate, the preacher,
who talks to me about The Way

as if it's the route he walks to work.
This writer too. His inspection
of notches in hands. Facial grooves.

He says you reach depths through the surface.
So I will lay the glistening surfaces
over my bunk and watch while he tries

not to look at those sides of beef
on the moor. And after I've re-sealed the envelope
and we've both settled again into our roles,

the silence in this cell will be loud enough
to throb in the preacher's ear
as he pushes through that last gate

and goes back down The Way,
smiling a little at our latest breakthrough,
at the miraculous progress on my case.

On the far side of the wall

My name is Margaret Tracey
And the fella I married's in jail

And he cries to me when I visit
That this prison they've sent him to rot in
Is a hole beyond the pale.

And he says he walks in shadows
On the other side of breath
For life is the sentence they gave him
But it feels a lot more like his death.

And my name is Margaret Tracey
And the bloke I married's in jail

And he cries when Visits are over
That mine is the only goodness
Amidst all his darkness and sin

Because the man he slain ain't sleeping
Though he felled him in cold blood.
No, his ghost creeps back every evening
and stares down at him in his bed.

And my name is Margaret Tracey
And the bloke I married's in jail

And I'm sick to my belly of Visits
With the guy who killed all my hope
Because he never said he needed me

When I was right there by his side.
And now distance is all that's between us
Though he claims he's loved me forever,
His *precious*, his own *beauteous*.

My name is Margaret Tracey
And I'm glad my husband's in jail.

And the fella he killed had it coming
Though his wife never harmed a soul's hair
And it's a funny old thing, sure I know

But it's his widow who walks here beside me
When I creep out of jail through this gate,
Into what they say are these *choices*
Though they feel a lot more like my fate.

Ancient Welsh Poetry

I have been lips waiting to be kissed
I have been the arrival that never came
I have been the silence that goes by no name
I have been all the things I ever missed

I have been a football searching for a boot
I have been a sheep parted from its flock
I have been the key that won't fit its lock
I have been the seed that never took root

I have been a train fastened to its track
I have been an anchor groaning on its chain
I have been the dry grass calling up for rain
I have been the nothing in the place between the cracks

I have been the pool longing to be wave
I have been the stillness before it turns to wind
I have been the thought so pure it never sinned
I have been all the gifts I never gave.

Drama

At last it happens. Screams on the landing
outside our class, cons rushing past, shaking
fists and bats. 'It's kicked off,' says the lad
at the back. His eyes burn. But others among us
shrink to dots. Then a teacher bursts through,
spilling laughs in her hands. 'Sorry,' she gasps.
'Got carried away. Me and the drama lads.
A knife-fight in *Macbeth*!' The actors troop back
along the landing, props bristling in their fists,
some whooping, one pretending with a mobile.
Their teacher composes herself. 'It's a new version,
up-to-date. Still loads of murder, but no castle –
just drugs on an estate. The working title's
Smack Death. What do you guys reckon?'

The painted ones

'There were blacks in England
before the English ever came:

'Moroccans shivering their bollocks off
on Hadrian's Wall. Centurions

for the Romans.' Lessons every day.
This one spoken by the white kid

who shot the Pakistani for a laugh.
'We were the Pritani then, mate.

That's the Greek name. Woad, see.
Blue dye. They daubed it on

to frighten invaders. Britons:
the painted ones. Not that it worked, like.

They still invaded!' Before I go,
he presses a book on me,

Maus by Art Spiegelman.
'It's all in there, pal –

prejudice. The stuff I done.'
I look back, grateful,

to find him lost in thought,
stroking the tattoos on his arm.

'A' level

So the exam day comes
and the daft bugger's on the roof.
They shout up at him:
'It's not worth it, lad –
your future's at stake!'
But it don't faze him.
'Send a screw up,'
he shouts, 'with the paper!
And no funny stuff!'
And that's where he sits it,
up there on the slates
with the fucking pigeons,
some idiot in a blazer
watching from the yard
with a big clock.
They reckon he passed too,
for what's it's worth.
Scraped a C,
Applied Maths.

Tale

Tell me about thunderstorms on cliffs,
how you opened your mouth to taste metal,
raced over dark fields, seeking
caves, overhangs, the hems of trees.

Tell me about ceilidhs: limestone walls,
a peat roof, how the fire burned red
and the bothey filled with smoke
and you breathed it in and the people danced.

Tell me what I have to guess,
how your love of being free
took you beyond the camp fire's ring of light,
brought you here, to a tin plate and sodium sky.

Tell me you didn't do it,
that you shouldn't be here.
Tell me the seconds, the minutes,
the hours, the days, the years.

Comfort

Sometimes catastrophe comforts.
Here's the difference between you and us:
where you see prisoners, we see ghosts.

They spin in shafts of light on landings. Motes.
Dust. The rain spoils even bars with rust.
Sometimes catastrophe comforts.

Let go of the dreams you sport.
This swamp we're in was once a forest.
You see streets and buses, I see glades. Ghosts.

When it starts to do my nut, I picture the court
which sentences every last thing to dust.
Sometimes catastrophe comforts.

From this cell window, I take my sport
with the girls who click up Sherwood Rise. Lust,
you say? It ain't their bodies. I see ghosts.

All high heels will soon wear low.
We do our time. And time undoes us.
Lasses now, but one day ghosts.
Sometimes catastrophe comforts.

Pleasure

The kind old lady who ran the B&B
near the jail was telling me about her war:

how, as a clippie, she travelled London
on double-deckers. 'Like a dream,'

she said. 'Like being free. Imagine, lad –
queen of the bus. *Me*. Doling tickets!'

Later, kids and the smallest county changed things,
but the city streets still led to her door.

She remembered the lodger she offered
a key to. His first night Out

and he passed up the chance. 'Her Majesty's
open prisons give you keys,' he explained,

'but I missed this thing they won't allow.
Hopping up door-steps to press the bell.'

A few pints on, he smiled when she answered
his ring: 'Sometimes the small things are enough.'

Later, on the same bed where the freed man
must have laid, I drift through Rutland's sleep:

empty streets and wind in summer trees,
birds singing to a lake and the guitarist

trying to crack some old Black Sabbath dirge.
Tomorrow – a job interview, and change

but for now, give me these rough old chords
and an open window. Small things. Enough.

The route of the arrow

It was midnight at the end of a long, humid June day and I was heading home up Elm Grove, the long tree-lined avenue that connects Brighton to its race course. In the distance, someone was shouting angrily, but I dismissed it as the usual outpourings from the malign local ley line that is sometimes mistakenly called London Road.

It had grown dark now under the elms, and muggy, and I was switching a heavy satchel from shoulder to shoulder as I traipsed up the hill. The satchel contained dozens of poems and stories by life prisoners. The work was to become an anthology and was currently at proof stage, its pages scarred by the red ink that I'd applied in my role as editor.

Earlier that day, I'd used the prisoners' work to illustrate a one-off session on writing and freedom at a local university. It had come as a refreshing change to be invited to teach in a peaceful environment, without the roar of confined men in the background, and I was reflecting upon the experience as I trudged up Elm Grove, watching the first shivers of summer lightning pass across the sky.

In the moments before the attack happened, I dimly recall that I was also thinking of trees, for Elm Grove is rich in them, its steep gradient a purpose-built parade route for the dead of Brighton, who are saluted by the elms on their final journey up the hill to the graveyard.

Back then, I was preoccupied by trees. During my year at the jail, I'd often found myself staring into the vast places within the jail's cherry tree. There had been something about the plight of this fruitful tree that reminded me of the prisoners I taught.

Maybe I also had more prosaic things on my mind as I traipsed home up the hill – the work on the satchel of proofs that awaited me, the struggle to find a job that provided enough to live on while continuing to write.

Whatever I was truly thinking vaporised as soon as I saw the ashen-faced man hurling beer bottles into the driveway of the local primary school.

His girlfriend clung to the school railings, clutching a toddler to her chest. The toddler howled in terror while she screamed at her boyfriend to stop.

The man did not stop. He went on ripping bottle after bottle from a carrier bag and hurling each of them into the gateway. The noise that came out of him while he did this was the most frightening I've ever heard. It was the roar of some forest beast, some dreadful thing gored by a trap. He was screaming so hard that his lips had turned blue, that his eyes seemed about to burst from their skull.

I was frightened, even, by his hair, a fierce buzz-cut that laid bare a bolt of bone across the back of his head. He was like a door that had been sealed from outside. We were stuck inside his rage with him, no way out.

When I attempted eye contact with his girlfriend, she shrank from my gaze and tightened her grip on the toddler. The toddler squirmed like a fish in a net, opening its lungs to gasp, gone beyond screaming into a racked silence. When I look back now, I see the child's eyes, I see the summer lightning that trembled beyond the trees.

Earlier that evening, I had talked about outlaws and arrows. I'd told the university students what jail had taught me: that certain men are like arrows, fired many years ago and falling to earth ever since. I'd learned that nothing can stop these arrows from falling, and that the only defence is to avoid the place where the arrow lands.

Now I had come to that place.

I said to the man: 'Steady, mate. Go easy. The school-kids...'

He'd hit me before I even saw him raise his hand. And I was down in the broken glass suffering his kicks while his fingers seemed still to be curling into a fist.

Who did I think I was, he asked me.

Who.

Did.

I.

Think.

I.

Was.

With each blow, I flew further from pain. The only experience I can compare it to is being rolled by an Atlantic wave. You don't know which way is up, which way is down. The roar of the ocean surrounds your body, but you are somehow separate from it. You have fallen into a gap between two worlds.

Then, somehow, I'd been flung clear and was wedged in a stand of privet bushes, using my satchel as a shield while he threw down punch after punch and I begged him to stop and his girlfriend screamed and the toddler burst free from her grip and toppled into the broken glass.

But I no longer cared about the child because the man had hit the satchel so hard that its catch had exploded and the prisoners' work was blowing free across the road. And he had taken a broken bottle in his fist and was telling me exactly how he intended to punish me for coming between him and his family. A private matter. And his voice had taken on a lower, more controlled, tone.

'Want some, do you. Want some.'

'Please,' I said. 'Your child...'

Lightning flashed through the trees behind him. It sounds like a cliché to say this. But all violence is a cliché, anyway. That's what I remember thinking as he stood above me under the lovely darkness of the elms with the broken bottle cocked like a gun in his fist. All violence is a cliché, anyway.

How I stumbled free, I don't recall. Why he chose to batter me from then on with his left hand rather than the hand with the bottle, I have no idea. I remember grovelling in the road for the prisoners' proofs while he kicked me, and stuffing the pages into my broken satchel, and realising that my attacker had cut his fist on its buckle, and his blood was dripping off my chin.

But then I was bolting up the hill past the Exhaust & Battery Centre, trying to breathe again, muttering my shame under my breath while he screamed somewhere behind me that there was no point running because he knew exactly where I lived.

And what hurt most was the exultant tone in his voice and the thought that I had given him exactly what he wanted and the memory of being squashed inside a stupid bush, and how I'd grovelled in the dirt while he kicked me.

And, although I later tried to comfort myself by putting it down to the injustice of a country where the rich are too rich and the poor too poor, and the schizophrenia of a town which is equal parts soother and savage, I knew I wasn't kidding myself.

For there isn't any comfort for a grown man who has been humiliated like a child in the street, not even when he bursts through the front door of his home and submits to the tenderness of his wife.

Joy of the mountains

is what the Greeks meant by 'oregano',
and it's here with me now in the loose rocks
of these high slopes at Europe's southern tip,

where waves filch the mountains' pockets
and freedom forces thoughts of jail on me:
spuds piled like stones, beans hardening on plates.

'The plan: to do us in on our own gas,
which happened, once – in the good old days!'
The con stirs his mug's black tarn, says: 'By the way,

the name for gassed air is *mephitic*' –
and stares at the place where that word will hang
and stale — knowledge going nowhere, like lists

learned by the lifer who's burned his time
swotting Classics, who knows all the Greek heroes,
yet hasn't walked in a meadow for years,

whom I'm trying to forget now as I test
a wall of scree, eyes watching from eyries
as I grope for a trail through the joy.

New in town

They make little jokes before sips, raise glasses
to hide funnies. Their girlfriends giggle. Wet lips.
You bring them close; all loneliness has its uses.

So find a place to stand at the long bar!
And tap a shoe on the rail – but spare yourself
the whistling, and don't look in the mirror
or at the girl becoming nude under the nuts.

Prepare a half-smile for the sudden laugh
while ignoring the dampness of your sleeve,
and nod slowly at a thing not said,
inspecting your wrist as if it's a watch…

till your eyes meet their eyes, and – Bang. The door.
Then turn your gaze to its draught, mistaking
strangers for friends you can't help but expect.

Visitation

The jail visits me in strange places:
on a wild Sardinian headland
where we shower outdoors
behind a mesh screen
under the pines

and feet come and go after dark
yet each caravan is empty
and ours is the only tent.
The owner shrugs, bare-chested,
when we describe those noises,

and we notice his skin,
greyed by prison tattoos:
a couple of crosses,
something like a tombstone
and arrows bursting hearts,

then the plague of tiny scars
that score his torso's length,
none very deep, or longer
than an inch, but each one
straight and true,

carved perhaps with a peck of glass
hidden for years from jailers –
the work of a man
who needs the sort of pain
he can put his fingers on.

That night, branches crack
on the deserted paths
of the campsite,
as if some restless thought
is circling our sleep,

while we lie, uneasy,
on the roots and needles
of his strange peninsula,
gripping the tent's zip,
like nurses over a wound.

Longing

to go back to the fields
that I pulled turnips from

to eat on the frozen days
when there were no lifts

to towns down the coast
where I wanted to find a way

to live with myself
after what I'd done

to people I loved
and what they'd done

to me, for we were none of us
angels, and ain't yet.

To go back and find that town
I was always wanting.

To stand on the roadsides
with all my hunger.

To live again through the bad times.

To go back to the bad times.

For the murdered

There isn't a phone card
in this whole jail that could reach you,

no bib-card on any door
with your name on it.

You're less than the sunken part
of an unmade bunk,

kicked-off sheets
that used to be warm.

You aren't anywhere now –
your voice

just an echo
in looks, shrugs,

turnings and rollings
over a pillow

in the dawn hours
when other sounds have gone

and, at last, across a distance
of field and street and bed,

your killers hear you,
calling, calling.

The unsaid

After I'd finished working at the prison, a recurring dream visited me.

My job had been to help inmates with their self-expression. Many of my students had done the worst thing a man can do, rape and murder, but I was rarely threatened, except by the place itself, which frightened me with its acrid smells and its hard, mustard walls. Yet I couldn't escape the dream, which came on and off for years, and was almost always the same in most details:

I had come home from work to find my partner gone, and only a stranger in our house. The stranger seemed to be a former prisoner, but I didn't recognise him. He was sitting on our settee, staring ahead, the TV playing without the volume up, a habit of the British that I've always hated and been susceptible to myself. There was nothing else in the dream, no violent act, no sense that the prisoner meant me harm, just an absence at the heart of the dream which made my heart pound.

'Where is she?' I asked the stranger.

He said nothing, just stared at the quiet television.

It was a dream structured like certain kinds of contemporary short stories, the meaning in the gaps, any significant action implied rather than spelled out. Much left unsaid, many things disguised. A lot of white space.

It was also one of those dreams that returns suddenly in the middle of the day, when you're busy on an errand in town, paying a bill at the bank or rushing to make a train, also a dream that played on many of my unanswered questions about what the men had done. Few told me their crimes, and I never asked. Hence, there was often an absence in my dealings with the students, a hole at the centre of our relationship which often seemed more real than the stuff that surrounded it: the classes, the tutorials.

It took a long time for the dream to release me from its grip. It took six years.

And then one day I was rushing for my train across a flat part of Brighton known as the Level, where all paths cross, when I heard a familiar voice greet me just as I approached the 'X' in the centre of the park.

Similar things have happened to me on other occasions: an old girlfriend suddenly appearing in the wrong place, an ex-colleague turning up in a new building... But this was the first time I'd seen one of the lifers on the Out.

'In a dream,' he smiled.

'Yeah...'

'And rushing, eh?'

'As usual. To work...'

'I heard you were staying here, but I didn't expect to see you,' he said. 'How are you doing?'

Heard from whose mouth? I thought, looking into his eyes for as long as I dared. They were a generous green, some mysterious gentleness in their depths for all the frowning they'd known. As his teacher, I had known the man's poetry: skilful, yearning lyrics that spoke of a former life on the road, whisky swigged from cans in smoky botheys, waves crashing ashore, foxes barking in the pastures. Of all the men I'd taught, he was the one who most confused me, the best writer, the prisoner who was kindest, and the man who also carried the biggest store of potential and had shown me the sharpest anger.

'I've been okay,' I said. 'Yourself?'

His smile faded just a little. 'You know. Adjusting.'

'It must be hard,'

'This?' he said. 'This is okay. I've known worse than this.'

'Yes.'

'My mobile number,' he said, and held it between us, carefully placed on his palm, a holy wafer.

I gazed around the Level, as if for help. This wasn't unusual for me, though normally I sought a more philosophical kind of support from the old place. The name of the Level often puts me in mind of those early anarchist organisations that once struggled to create a more equal world. I rarely cross its scrubby patch of green without thinking of the Levellers. And, frequently, this sends my doggy mind wandering into all sorts of reveries: hopes for a better world, fears of the violence that usually bring about change, long conversations with myself about what I'd do if there was a chance to change things. Whether I'd fight or flee.

Today, as always, boys were kicking balls, drunks squawking, young mothers nursing babies. There it all was. The free world. Everything that the prisoner must have longed for, and hoped to find miracles in. Was he disappointed in what he'd found? Or had it met his expectations?

I still couldn't meet the man's gaze. Ahead, the elms were lovely and full, the last of their kind in England, the South Downs a barrier against the insects that preyed upon them. Under those elms, a fortnight previously, in the road between the Caroline of Brunswick pub and the entrance to the Level, I had been a member of a crowd that had watched a young woman die. She was the victim of a hit and run, a young person with her life ahead of her, who had breathed her last in public view under the shimmering trees.

In the prison, I had taught hit and run merchants, men who had struck blameless pedestrians in vehicles they had stolen. This had been on my mind as I watched the medics trying to save the girl under the elms. It was on my mind now as the man waited for me to take his mobile number from him.

Violence. In those days, after I'd worked with men accused of causing death and harm to others, it was never far from my thoughts, if you could dignify that incoherent tumble of emotions with a word as noble as 'thought'.

As the released man stood there waiting for me to return his generosity, I swirled with all the fears that had been stirred up by the prison.

The Level isn't far from the road where I was beaten up by the deranged man with the broken bottle, and I was still a little nervous when I crossed the open spaces nearby, even though I knew that the chances of meeting again with a random attacker were extremely slight.

Bullying works in that illogical way, and most of its practitioners realise that. It isn't the bully's war that destroys you – it's the war he sets off in your head. I knew this from the period of bullying I'd endured at school, each lunchtime a humiliation, but the nights far worse: full of waking nightmares and wet beds.

Most men never really get over that stuff. It was perhaps one of the reasons I'd gone out of my way to get a job in prison, in a place that scared me to the roots. I think I must have wanted to study violent people at close-quarters, and to try to work out why I'd been bullied. What there was in some men that they needed to inflict harm? What there was in me that attracted it?

It wasn't fair on the released man, of course. Even when I'd once inadvertently upset him, he'd never hit me, never threatened me in any way. If I'd made him an emblem of those bad things, it was my own doing, a demonisation that I'd have found detestable in others.

So there we were, standing upon the Level, each ablaze with his own thoughts.

And, at last, I put the note in my pocket, and the waiting man left a gap for me to pass my number back to him.

But, instead of doing so, I gave him a forced smile and said goodbye and went to get my train.

A wise woman once said to me: 'The biggest question in your life is: how much pain will you allow yourself to experience?'

I thought about that as I escaped across the street where I'd seen the girl die.

Then the elms healed themselves around me, and the lifer and the Level were gone.

On the train to work, a young lad talked excitedly about knives through all the stations between East Worthing and Barnham.

There was a question in my head. It went round and round all day: No matter the pain it may cause, is it ever okay to turn away someone who needs you?

I wanted to be free of the jail.

I wanted to be gone.

The Bright Forest

Such did they name it,
thinking of light's glare
on leaves
and the sap's teem
from root to tip.

Under its groves,
they piled stones
to mark their kingdoms
and raised mounds
for their dead.

They called it Thynghowe,
sacred ground
for the parliament
where they gathered
to heal their scars.

It isn't far
across the estates
and arterial roads from that place
to this. Follow the glare.
Take care on the crossings.

[Sherwood's name is thought to stem from Old English, scir – bright,
wudu – wood]

Hit and run

They dismantled the shrine this morning –
either that, or the last of the wilted flowers
was washed away by a summer downpour.
Now it's just an ordinary garden
outside the bar where he hurled his car
at your life, where your body was flung
to the white line, medics crouched in a ring
when I passed moments later, the trees
swaying over your head as they beat
your chest, a crowd drawn to the sirens
and lights, some strange grace in their silence,
in the wind that bent the boughs as you lay dying,
the light that shimmered in the elms and oaks,
those mute witnesses in their long coats.

Apology

Made thieves of my eyes,
counted possessions,
listed your books, their contradictions.
Looked at your hands
while you tried to find my eyes,
missed it all by looking too hard.
Thought I was a searchlight,
I was just another wall.

Some further reading

Some of these books allowed me understanding of prison life (and of states of mind that may prevail during confinement). Others helped to open up inmates' writing.

Gate Fever by James Campbell (Sphere)
Orphans by Charles D'Ambrosio (Clear Cut Press)
Poems from Guantanamo ed. Marc Falkhoff (University of Iowa Press)
Wild Mind by Natalie Goldberg (Bantam)
The Grass Arena by John Healy (Penguin)
Poetry in the Making by Ted Hughes (Faber)
A Life Inside: A Prisoner's Notebook by Erwin James (Guardian Books)
The Home Stretch: from Prison to Parole by Erwin James (Guardian Books)
Seek by Denis Johnson (Harper Perennial)
Angels by Denis Johnson (Harper Perennial)
Hard on the Knuckle by Chris Jones (Smith Doorstop)
The Safe House by Chris Jones (Shoestring Press)
The Prisons Handbook by Mark Leech (Waterside Press)
Sectioned by John O'Donoghue (John Murray)
The Courage of his Convictions by Tony Parker & Robert Allerton (Arrow)
Life after Life: Interviews with Twelve Murderers by Tony Parker (Pan)
Doing Time: 25 Years of Prison Writing – PEN anthology (Arcade)
Prisongate: the Shocking State of Prisons by Sir David Ramsbotham (Free Press)
Why Did I Ever by Mary Robison (Counterpoint)
Writing Poems by Peter Sansom (Bloodaxe)
Invisible Crying Tree by Tom Shannon & Christopher Morgan (Doubleday)
Wormwood by Ken Smith (Bloodaxe)
Criminal Conversations: an Anthology of Tony Parker, ed. Keith Soothill (Routledge)
Disguised as a Poem: My Years Teaching at San Quentin by Judith Tannenbaum (Northeastern University Press)
The Speakers by Heathcote Williams (Robin Clark Ltd.)
Above the River by James Wright (Bloodaxe)